WHY

CHRISTIANS

SIN

Discovery House

P U B L I S H E R S
BOX 3566 · GRAND RAPIDS, MI 49501

*PUBLISHING BOOKS THAT FEED
THE SOUL WITH THE WORD OF GOD.*

WHY
CHRISTIANS
SIN

Avoiding the Dangers
of an Uncommitted Life

J. Kirk Johnston

Unless indicated otherwise, Scripture is taken from the NEW
AMERICAN STANDARD BIBLE, Copyright © 1960, 1962, 1963,
1968, 1971, 1972, 1973, 1975, 1977 by The Lockman Foundation.

Johnston, James Kirkland, 1956
    Why Christians sin : Avoiding the Dangers of an
    Uncommitted Life / James Kirkland Johnston.
        p. cm.
    Includes bibliographical references.
    ISBN 0-929239-51-2
    1. Sin. 2. Salvation. 3. Sanctification. I. Title.
  BT715.J64   1991
  241'.3—dc20   91-24870
                                   CIP

Discovery House Publishers is affiliated with Radio Bible Class,
Grand Rapids, Michigan.

Discovery House books are distributed to the trade by Thomas
Nelson Publishers, Nashville, Tennessee 37214.

Printed in the United States of America

92 93 94 95 96 /   / 10 9 8 7 6 5 4 3 2

To my parents who encouraged me,
to my dear wife Gayle who supported me,
and to the men of Harmony Bible Church who
faithfully prayed for this project for over three years.

Contents

**PART 4: WHY CHRISTIANS SIN—
THE LACK OF SPIRITUAL EXERCISE**

PART 5: WHEN CHRISTIANS SIN

FOREWORD

Whenever I am asked in an open question and answer session what I consider to be the greatest need of the church today, I invariably answer with words like dedication, holiness, commitment, and godliness. Often that does not satisfy the questioner, for usually he or she wants an issue-related response rather than a character-oriented one. But in my judgment lack of commitment among God's people remains the number one problem in the church.

This book addresses that need head on. While it is a book on discipleship and Christian living, it avoids quick fixes, gimmicks, formulas, and fads, which seem to be all that some such books offer. This one presents a "meat and potatoes" approach to avoiding the dangers of an uncommitted life.

The work is so well-balanced that no one who follows its guildlines could fail to experience a stronger and more stable Christian walk. Emphasis is given both to the need for understanding certain basic doctrines as well as to the importance of healthy spiritual exercises. This balance reflects the author's good theology combined with his years of experience in the pastorate.

Individuals will profit from reading it; groups will be helped by studying it; congregations will be strengthened by hearing its message preached.

—Charles C. Ryrie

PREFACE

A recent Gallup poll claims that many Americans have faith in God but their faith doesn't make much of a difference in their lives.[1] Many of these Americans go to evangelical churches, yet they are indistinguishable from non-Christians! What is going on?

Some Christians, popularly referred to as "Lordship Salvation" advocates, say that many, if not all of these professing Christians, are not genuine believers. These people are just "professors, but not possessors." Others, known as "Grace" proponents, maintain that many of these professing "Christians" are true believers. The problem, they say, is that some Christians have a desire to live for God and to do what is right but others don't and never will. In addition, there are still others who believe that true Christians can either lose their faith or lose their salvation, or both.

All of these explanations attempt to explain why so many people today profess to be Christians but consciously sin, or live, as Paul says, like "mere men" (1 Cor. 3:3). Christians are often confused about all these explanations. I hope my book will provide some answers by showing from God's Word why many Christians are not experiencing significant spiritual growth and instead are consciously sinning.

I believe many professing Christians are genuine believers who want to live for God and do what is right; however, they need help to get back on the right track. My desire is to see these believers helped and their lives changed. Obviously, God has to work or all is for naught. But I know that God is working, and I trust He will work through this book to make a difference in peoples' lives for His glory!

ACKNOWLEDGEMENTS

Dr. Gary McIntosh, Dr. Boyd Luter, Tina Whitaker, and all those at Biola University who encouraged me to write this book.

To Robert DeVries for his willingness to publish a book from a young, unknown pastor from Iowa.

To Carol Holquist for her professional help, but more importantly, her encouraging phone calls that kept me going.

To the elders of Harmony Bible Church who generously allowed me the time to work on this book.

To Paul Hillman who is not only an excellent editor but a friend as well.

To the staff and secretaries of Harmony Bible Church who humored me by letting me think that I knew what I was doing.

To Dr. Charles Ryrie who knows me well and still graciously consented to write the foreword.

To Dr. Bob Saucy, the primary adviser for my doctoral dissertation, who constantly exhorted me above all else to be true to God and His Word.

PART 1

HOW CHRISTIANS SIN

CHAPTER 1

SALVATION AND SIN

One of my college classmates, a minister, robbed fourteen banks! I couldn't believe it. We were not close friends, but we had classes together, sat near one another in chapel occasionally, and played basketball on the same team in a local tournament. He was even the associate pastor of a church I attended for a while.

Why did he rob the banks? To finance dates with prostitutes. He is now serving time in prison for his crimes. Anyone who knew him at all was shocked by his behavior. Like the proverbial guy next door, he just didn't seem like the type to do something this terrible and sordid.

Almost every Christian knows someone who has professed Christ and has manifested what seemed to be real spiritual fruit but is now willfully and knowingly sinning. These disturbing situations raise a lot of questions and sometimes sow doubts in our minds. We long for biblical answers for them and for ourselves; we want to understand what is going on and how to get these Christians back on the right track.

When Christians consciously sin over significant periods of time, we either assume they were never truly saved or that they have "turned their backs on God" and are no longer saved. While I recognize that people can be "professors but not possessors" and that people can lose their faith according to some Christians, I am convinced that many sinning Christians are truly born again—even the pastor who robbed fourteen banks.

Is it possible for Christians to willfully and knowingly sin over a long period of time? And if so, how is it possible?

OUR INITIAL DESIRE

Let's go back to the beginning, to when a person first becomes a Christian. As R. C. Sproul has said, "Every Christian should have a passion to please God. We are to delight in honoring Him. It is our own greatest pleasure to please our Redeemer. We all begin the Christian life with the intention of living in such a way as to please Him."[1]

No verse explicitly states that we begin our Christian lives with the intention of pleasing God; nevertheless, theologically and logically this statement can be proven beyond reasonable doubt.

For us to live for God, we need both the ability and the desire. Before we came to Christ, we had neither; but the moment that we trusted Christ as Savior, the Holy Spirit came to live within us. Romans 8:8–9 says that we "who are in the flesh cannot please God. However, [we] are not in the flesh but in the Spirit, if indeed the Spirit of God dwells in [us]. But if [we do not] have the Spirit of God, [we do] not belong to Him."

These verses teach that true Christians have "the Spirit of Christ" dwelling within them as soon as they "belong to Him." Furthermore, according to Philippians

2:13, God works in them "to will and to work for His good pleasure." God is at work in Christians urging them to do His will and enabling them to do it. The Holy Spirit undoubtedly accomplishes this, and no good reason exists for placing this work after salvation. Rather, from believers' spiritual conceptions and infancies, the Spirit is working in their lives to influence and enable them to do what is right. What's more, newborn Christians themselves should desire to do what is right.

For people to be born again, they have to be convinced that they are sinners who deserve eternal condemnation. Otherwise, they have no need of a Savior. If people only understand that they were lost and headed for hell, and now because of Christ are headed for heaven, these two truths alone should be enough to cause them to want to do what God wants them to do. Even non-Christians are capable of being grateful. How much more those who are new creatures in Christ (2 Cor. 5:17).

Therefore, at the moment of salvation, new Christians will have the ability and the desire to grow spiritually and please God.

A further confirmation of this initial desire is found in Hebrews 5. In this chapter, the writer of Hebrews addressed immature Christians who had been believers long enough that they should have been teaching others (v. 12), but instead they were still "babes" in need of milk (v. 13). The writer said that they had "become dull of hearing" (v .11). The term *dull of hearing* means that the Hebrew Christians had become "slow or lazy in regard to spiritual matters." Note this is what they *had become*, and it "was not the case with them originally."[2] Like all Christians, the Hebrew believers started out with the desire to follow Christ and to grow spiritually; however, something happened along the way.

WILLING BUT UNABLE

Although Christians may be willing to serve God, they may not always have the strength to follow their spiritual desires. In 1 Thessalonians 5:14 Paul said to "encourage the faint-hearted." The term "faint-hearted" means literally "the small souled."[3] This refers to Christians, who because of their background or immaturity, struggle in regard to faith in God. They have a difficult time believing that God can or will do certain things in their lives. The Spirit is leading them to do what is right, but they struggle with accepting the fact that God really can help them to conquer their sin and live victoriously. Their faith is genuine, but it is weak and immature. They are chained to the past, as Josh McDowell illustrated:

> We're like a circus elephant tied down by a bicycle chain. We ask how one small chain could hold a powerful elephant. The trainer explains that the chain doesn't hold him; it's the elephant's memory that keeps him from trying to escape.
>
> When the elephant was very young, he didn't have the strength to break the chain or pull free. He learned then that the chain was stronger than he was and he hasn't forgotten that. The result is that the elephant, now full grown and powerful, remembers only that he tried to break the chain and couldn't. So he never tries again. His memory, not the chain, binds him. Of course, occasionally an elephant does discover he can break the chain, and from then on his keeper has trouble controlling him.[4]

All Christians to a certain extent are victims of their past and are "faint-hearted." This is why the apostle Paul commanded the Ephesian Christians to "lay aside the old self," which was their "former manner of life"[5] (Eph.4:22). Paul wanted believers to strip off their sins like they took off clothing. Although a new Christian has for the most part "laid aside the old self with its evil practices" (Col. 3:9), some sins take determined effort to put aside (Eph. 4:25–31 and Heb. 12:1). Getting rid of stubborn sins will not be easy; but if Christians determine to take them off, with God's help they can do it! Even though some new believers appear to be unwilling to deal with sin and make Christ Lord of their lives, in reality they are simply "faint-hearted" and will require encouragement.

A gifted evangelist once shared a story with me about a woman who trusted Christ one night during one of his evangelistic crusades. The next day leaders from a local church went to her home to help her in her new walk with Christ. However, she would not let them in the door, let alone talk with them. They weren't sure what was going on, but they were persistent and continued for a number of days to go to her home. Each time she refused to talk with them. After several rejections, they were finally admitted to her home, and she explained to them why she had refused to see them. She had put her trust in Christ the night she heard the gospel; and she wanted to do what was right, but she was living with a man who was not her husband. She struggled with telling him to leave for several days, which is why she did not want to visit with them. She knew what she was doing was wrong. The Spirit was urging her to correct the situation, and she finally did. Was this woman willing from the very beginning of her conversion to have Christ as Lord of her life? I think so. The very fact that she struggled with her situation and ultimately did what was right is a very definite indication that she did want Christ to be her Lord, as well as her Savior.

I trust this lady has continued to live for the Lord, but what if she has gone back to her lover after several years? What could have happened to cause her to stop following Christ and doing what's right? After all, the Holy Spirit is working in the believer's life. Doesn't the Holy Spirit keep Christians from sinning?

CHAPTER 2

THE SPIRIT AND UNKNOWN SIN

A few years ago I was in a meeting with fellow pastors and I heard an incredible but true story. It was about a young man who was pursuing a very wild life-style. He was quite a "ladies' man," and he was constantly dating and sleeping with different women. Then one day he was confronted with the gospel message and responded in simple faith to the good news about Jesus Christ. His life immediately began to change in some very definite ways, but not in every way. He continued to date and sleep with a number of girlfriends. While doing so, he faithfully shared the gospel with all of them. Some of these girls apparently trusted Christ as a result!

Could the Holy Spirit really have been in this young man's life? Romans 8:14 states that "all who are being led by the Spirit of God, these are sons of God." In other words, everyone who is a son or daughter of God is being led by the Spirit. The object of this leading is righteousness. Every time believers are confronted by a decision to either sin or do what is right, the Spirit will always lead them toward righteousness and away from sin. Was this young man quenching the Spirit?

PUTTING OUT THE FIRE

In 1 Thessalonians 5:19, Paul commanded the Thessalonian Christians not to quench the Spirit. Apparently the Thessalonian Christians as a church were not receptive to those in their midst who had the gift of prophecy. In fact, they were actually "despising" these prophecies, rather than accepting them as being from the Spirit (v.20). The word *quench* refers to the putting out of a fire or light, and fire is associated with prophecy in the Old Testament (Jer. 20:9). Therefore, some conclude that to "quench the Spirit" is simply to reject the gift of prophecy or Spirit-inspired prophecies.[1] In other words, "quenching the Spirit" is a specific type of sin.

While rejecting Spirit-inspired prophecies *is* a sin, there is a greater principle taught here regarding the Holy Spirit and sin in general. Fire in the New Testament is also associated with the general activity of the Spirit, not just prophecy (Matt. 3:11; Acts 2:3–4; Rom. 12:11). Is it possible that Christians could quench the Spirit in other areas of His ministry? There is no logical reason to deny this possibility. In rejecting the prophecies given by the Spirit, the Thessalonians were not only suppressing the Spirit's work in their lives, but ultimately they also were resisting God's will (1 Thess. 5:18). If Christians are able to quench God's Spirit and thus resist God's will in one area, what is there to keep them from doing it in other areas as well?

Charismatic or Pentecostal leaders might say that those with a "second blessing" would never "quench the Spirit." However, some of these same leaders have fallen into sin themselves. This does not mean they are

22

unbelievers or that the Spirit has departed from them; but if they have resisted God's will, they are quenching the Spirit. Since all Christians sin (1 John 1:8), all Christians "quench the Spirit."

But exactly how long can a Christian say "no" to the Spirit and continue to sin? A close look at 1 Thessalonians 5:19 indicates that the Thessalonians had been suppressing God's Spirit for some indefinite period of time.[2] Exactly how long Paul does not say, but his letter proves Christians do quench the Spirit at times, and this quenching is not necessarily a momentary happening.

Arguing for continously sinning believers makes some Christians and theologians get very uncomfortable. Doesn't the Bible teach in Philippians 2:13 that "God is effectually and continuously at work in the life of the believer?"[3] This verse does indicate that God is the One who initiates all good and righteous behavior in believers. He provides the impetus for right living through His Spirit who indwells them. Any desire to do what is good ultimately comes from the Spirit.

God also continually supplies the ability or energy to do what is good. The word *work* in Philippians 2:13 may mean to "produce or effect,"[4] and God's supernatural power is the cause; but Paul was not saying that God actually forces or irresistibly causes the believer to do His will. Even those who state that spiritual growth is dependent on the grace of God are forced to concede that Christians can indeed hinder or slow down the process.[5]

How much or how long can a true Christian thwart the process of spiritual growth? The Bible does not say specifically. Even though God is powerfully working in believers through His Spirit, they can still choose to sin for indefinite, but significant periods of time. But why would a Christian want to quench the Spirit and sin?

UNKNOWN TERRITORY

Christians can resist God's Spirit unknowingly. Whenever Christians sin, the Spirit will be working in their lives to convict them and to encourage them to do what is right. However, believers may mistake the Spirit's convicting work for an overly sensitive conscience. In this case, Christians may continue in certain sins until God's Word confronts them, objectively confirming the convicting work of the Spirit.

Someone might say that someone who has been saved for some time will not sin unknowingly. People who have been Christians for years and know God's Word will know when they are quenching the Spirit. However, mature Christians can sin unconsciously, especially when an activity is in one of the so-called gray areas. The Bible does not explicitly condemn certain activities, but they may well be sins in certain situations.

One example is owning a VCR. Some Christians believe that these machines are always sinful because, among other things, people can bring pornography right into their homes and watch it in privacy. The problem with this line of thinking is that owning a VCR is not listed in Scripture as a sin, and God knew that these devices would be invented and available in this century. The reason God does not generally or specifically prohibit VCR's is because, for some Christians, VCRs can be very edifying. For instance, they give Christians the ability to tape quality television programs. Nevertheless, not every Christian should own a VCR. For some a VCR could be a tremendous temptation to sin.

It is also possible for Christians to commit sins unknowingly when a particular sin is considered acceptable by other Christians. Certain sins are generally considered acceptable in certain cultures. For instance, Paul listed greed as a sin (Rom. 1:29). Among believers in the Soviet Union greed is still considered to be a serious sin. However, in the American evangelical community, greed is usually considered a sin only if it is too conspicuous. There are other examples, but the point is that the Spirit's work may not be as effective as it should be because we unconsciously rationalize certain sins away when "everybody's doin' it." We may need the confirmation of God's Word in order to cease sinning.

God's Spirit leads toward righteousness and away from sin, but the Spirit normally works in conjunction with the written Word. It is erroneous to think that old or new Christians will be able to clean up their sinful lives with the Spirit's help, apart from a working knowledge of God's Word.

The sexually active young man who found Christ eventually dated and propositioned a girl from a local evangelical church. This got back to the elders of the church. They confronted him with the biblical prohibitions against fornication. When he saw from Scripture that he was committing sexual sin, he was genuinely repentant. He may have had some doubts about his behavior, but he didn't know these doubts came from the Holy Spirit. Until he saw the wrongness of his behavior confirmed in God's Word, he did not stop it.

Christians can say "no" to the Holy Spirit unknowingly, but does the Scripture also indicate that Christians can consciously resist the Spirit and willingly sin?

CHAPTER 3

THE FLESH AND CONSCIOUS SIN

O ne of the finest pastors I've ever known of decided one day that he wanted out of his marriage and ministry, so he very carefully devised a plan of escape. He drove his car into a nearby lake and made the scene appear as if he had drowned. Then he went off to start a new life and left his family and church to pick up the pieces of their shattered lives.

Some Christians are not really believers, and the lack of desire to do God's revealed will is an indication that this is the case. Charles Haddon Spurgeon reportedly warned his students that "if the professed convert distinctly and deliberately declares that he knows the Lord's will but does not mean to attend to it, you are not to pamper his presumption, but it is your duty to assure him that he is not saved."[1] However, personal experience and God's Word both teach that Christians can and do premeditatedly sin.

THE FLESH IS WEAK

Abraham was called "the friend of God" (James 2:23), and yet he lied about his relationship to Sarah, not once, but twice! (Gen. 12:10–20, 20:2–18). David was also called "a man after [God's own] heart" (Acts 13:22), but he committed adultery with Bathsheba and then tried to cover it up by having her husband murdered (2 Sam. 11). No one who takes God's Word seriously would question whether or not these men are now in the presence of God. They were great men of faith. However, they willfully and premeditatedly sinned.

Now someone might say that these men, as great as they were, did not have the Holy Spirit as all believers do today; and if they had possessed the Spirit, they would not have committed these sins. This sounds like a good point except for what Paul said in Romans 7:15, "For that which I am doing, I do not understand; for I am not practicing what I would like to do, but I am doing the very thing I hate."

Although some think Paul was talking about his experience as an unbeliever, Paul wrote Romans 7:14–25 in the present tense, emphatically referred to himself as "I," and recognized God's law in his inner man (v. 22). I think he was writing about his experience as a believer.

Having stated in 7:15 that he sometimes did exactly what he did not want to do and undoubtedly what he knows is wrong, Paul went on in verse 17 to identify the source of his problem. The source was the "sin" that indwelt him, or, as he says in verse 18, his "flesh." The term *flesh* refers numerous times in the Bible to the substance of which humans are made, but New Testament writers use the word to mean the source of sin. What ties these two meanings of *flesh* together is the fact that flesh is sinful because all human beings are sinful. The flesh works along with the world and Satan to tempt us to sin. As R. C. Sproul stated:

> The Flesh is an ally with the World. It seeks its justification not from the righteousness of Christ but from the standards of this world. The Flesh is allied with the World and the World is allied with Satan. Here the enemy seeks our destruction by calling us away from the Spirit to surrender to the Flesh.[2]

The flesh is certainly a source of sin in believers; but if Christians are new creatures in Christ, why or how could they ever knowingly or deliberately "surrender to the flesh?"

If the flesh is *more powerful* than the Spirit, then there is no problem in understanding why Christians end up sinning rather than doing what is right. If the flesh and the Spirit are *equal in power*, then again there is no problem understanding why Christians sometimes sin. However, most theologians and Christians would not be willing to say that the flesh is more powerful than the Spirit or even equal to the Spirit. After all, the Holy Spirit is God! (Acts 5:3–4; 2 Cor. 3:17). Therefore, in a battle between the flesh and the Spirit, the Spirit is going to win every time. When Christians are tempted to sin by the flesh, the Spirit is going to offer them more than enough power to resist. So the ultimate reason Christians consciously sin cannot be the "flesh," even though it is the source of sin, because the Spirit is continually offering them the power of God to do what is right.

If Christians "walk by the Spirit," they "will not carry out the desire of the flesh" (Gal. 5:16). This being the case, the reason that Christians knowingly or deliberately sin must be because they willingly choose to do so.

Now in spite of this truth, some still insist that the flesh is the ultimate, determining cause of sin in the believer. In his book, *Birthright*, David Needham stated that "a Christian can become so weak, so ignorant that the flesh level of his personhood, which is supposed to be his slave, rises up to act as his master."[3] Romans 7:20 certainly seems to indicate that this is so. Paul said, "but if I am doing the very thing I do not wish, I am no longer the one doing it, but sin which dwells in me." Yet if Paul was saying that the flesh sometimes overpowered him and forced him to sin, he was negating any responsibility for his own actions. He was declaring, "I'm human; therefore I can't do anything about it."

Needham was quick to say that "in the broadest sense of your personhood, you are fully responsible for your flesh."[4] But it doesn't matter how broadly you define one's personhood; if Christians can will to do what is right but be overruled by their flesh, they cannot reasonably be held accountable for their sins.

It seems like a lot of people today are trying to evade personal responsibility for their actions. One of my favorite examples is a guy down in Kentucky who was arrested for driving under the influence of alcohol. When his case came before the judge, the man pleaded not guilty. He explained that he was legally blind, and his dog barks to let him know when to stop and go at traffic lights. Therefore, he contended, the dog was the real driver of the vehicle and the dog was completely sober. Unfortunately for him, the judge failed to accept his defense and sentenced him to thirty days in jail anyway.

It is becoming increasingly popular in some Christian circles to attribute certain sins to demons. Some not only say that demons tempt Christians to sin in various ways but that demons actually cause Christians to sin! This line of thinking has little biblical support.[5] What's more, this kind of belief once again contradicts the biblical principle of personal responsibility (Jer. 31:29, 30).

Just as Christians should not say "the devil made me do it," they also should not say, "the flesh made me do it." The fact that Christians are sons and daughters of Adam is no excuse. Although Paul indicated that the flesh was the *source* of sinful desires in believers (Rom. 7:17, 20), he also taught that believers still make the ultimate choice about whether or not to act on those desires (Rom. 7:15, 19).

INADEQUATE ANSWERS

Why would Christians choose to sin rather than choose what they know God wants them to do?

Four answers are commonly given today.

First, some would point to Romans 8:16 and explain that Christians who willfully sin have forgotten their true identity as "children of God." While it is true that Christians can forget who they are and sin as a result, Christians can also be well aware of who they are and sin anyway.

Second, some say Christians choose to sin because they have lost sight of what God has done for them. Second Peter 1:9 indicates that Christians can be "blind or short-sighted, having forgotten [their] purification from [their] former sins." It is certainly possible for believers to lose sight of the wonderful things that God has done for them; and when this happens, they can sin willfully. I have counseled Christians who can recite all the wonderful things that God has done for them over a period of many years, but they decide to sin against Him anyway.

Third, some wisely state that Christians consciously choose to sin because they have forgotten that God will severely discipline disobedient believers. Sometimes Christians do forget the consequences of sin and this opens the door for disobedience. Just as people continue to eat, drink, and smoke things that they acknowledge are shortening their lives, Christians continue in certain sins, knowing that God will discipline them and that the discipline could be quite severe.

Recently a Christian woman called me and she was terribly distraught. She told me that her husband of many years was leaving her for a younger woman. She had confronted him about the wrongness of what he was doing and warned him that God might severely discipline him. As he was leaving, he told her that he knew that what he was doing was wrong and that God would probably take his life, but he was going to leave her anyway!

Fourth, some have said that Christians who consciously sin have lost their focus on the future. These Christians have forgotten that God will reward in heaven only those who have lived faithfully for Him here on earth (1 Cor. 9:24). Christians who fail to keep eternity in mind often sin in the here and now. A lady once told me that she "didn't care if she lived in the slums of heaven," as long as she was there. In many cases, Christians are not motivated to deal with sin simply to get rewards or commendations in heaven.

Although these four explanations may clarify why Christians sin temporarily or momentarily, none really explain why Christians choose to sin repeatedly over significant periods of time. Does something else happen to them?

CHAPTER 4

DISAPPOINTMENT AND WILLFUL SIN

A few years ago a prominent pastor I knew committed suicide. His death was totally unexpected and very disturbing. Even now the reasons for his action are quite unclear. Christians who knew him both in and outside of his church are either hurt or confused or both. Some are so hurt and confused that it has led them into conscious sin. A good friend of mine recently told me about a tragic example.

There is a businessman who really grew spiritually under this pastor and greatly respected him as a mature Christian. When this layman heard that this man of God committed suicide, he told my friend, "if he [the pastor] couldn't stick it out, then I can't either!" This believer started spending most of his time going to bars while his marriage and business disintegrated. His disappointment with the pastor led him away from God and down a path of despair.

DISILLUSIONMENT WITH OTHERS

Sometimes when Christians fail to live for God, other Christians looking on get quite disillusioned. This is particularly true when less mature believers are looking at more mature believers as an example to follow. When the "example" fails, the ones following may despair of ever being able to live the Christian life as well. At that point, these less mature believers may use the failure of the mature believers as an excuse to "throw in the towel," spiritually-speaking. They reason that if so-and-so cannot live successfully and faithfully for God, then neither can they! Of course, this is not a legitimate reason to stop trying and to start sinning, but some Christians do respond this way.

Sometimes disappointment leads to anger, particularly in the situations where it seems that the ones sinning are thoroughly enjoying themselves and punishment does not seem to be forthcoming. At that point, these disappointed Christians sometimes use the situation as an excuse to consciously sin themselves. This whole scenario was in danger of happening when Paul wrote his second letter to the believers in Thessalonica.

In 2 Thessalonians 3:13, Paul said to the Thessalonian Christians, "Do not grow weary of doing good." The words *do not grow weary* mean "not to lose courage or give up."[1] The Thessalonians had not given up on "doing good," but they were apparently in danger of doing so. From the context, it is clear that they were getting discouraged about fellow Christians who were leading undisciplined lives. This discouraging situation was enough to threaten their desire to keep doing what was "good."

What this passage indicates is that it is possible for Christians who are living for the Lord to get discouraged because of fellow Christians who are not, and this can lead them to stop doing what is "good." It can lead them to sin knowingly and willfully.

Of course, once again, this is not a legitimate excuse to sin, but people do use it.

Several years ago the church I now serve had some internal struggles. Some members saw what was happening and saw people sinning and became terribly disenchanted with the church. Some stopped going to church completely and are now consciously sinning in a number of ways. When confronted with their sin, they point back to the believers who failed so miserably years ago as the cause. Many of them are unwilling to admit at this point that the sin of others long ago does not excuse their sin today.

God's Word and experience indicate that true Christians can get discouraged with fellow believers and that this can lead them into conscious sin. Although a fact, it can never be a legitimate excuse for sin.

DISCOURAGEMENT WITH RESULTS

In Galatians 6:9, Paul urged the Galatian Christians "not [to] lose heart in doing good." In the context, Paul was urging the Galatians not to "grow weary" in supporting those who teach them God's Word (v. 6) and those who need help in "the household of the faith" (v. 10). However, Paul was also sharing with the Galatians a general principle about the Christian life pertaining to sowing and reaping. He encouraged them not to give up, even if they didn't see the harvest they were looking for right away. This passage in Galatians teaches that it is possible for Christians to get discouraged about a lack of results in the Christian life, and when believers get discouraged, this can lead them into conscious sin.

Now someone may rightly ask: Where do Christians' great enemies, the world, the flesh, and the Devil, fit into the process of willful sin? Normally Christians desire to do what is right not only because of what God has done for them but because they know that God's way is the path of blessing. This does not mean that Christians do not sin; God's Word indicates that they do so all the time (1 John 1:8). However, what they regularly do is sin unconsciously, even though they don't want to, and they try not to.

Anne Ortland in her book, *Children Are Wet Cement*, told of shopping with her son Nels for a shirt and finding one they liked that said "Shrink Resistant" on the collar. Nels asked the young clerk what that term meant, and the clerk said, "I think it means that the shirt does shrink, but it doesn't want to."[2]

That is how true Christians are much of the time, but when they get discouraged about a lack of results in their Christian lives, they become vulnerable to temptation from either the world, the flesh, or the Devil.

The world, the flesh, and the Devil do try to influence, seduce, and tempt Christians to sin. It is only when Christians are discouraged with fellow believers or the Christian life that they are willing to listen and give in.

MAD AT GOD

Can Christians be disappointed with fellow believers or the Christian life and *not* with God also? Perhaps, in the beginning, but logically and eventually their disappointment has to be with God as well. Why? Because God is ultimately in control of the situation. He is able to judge and correct the erring Christian. When one believer sees another sinning, the initial reaction is, "Why doesn't that person see his sin and get his act together?" Inevitably, however, if the situation continues, the question is, "Why doesn't God step in and do something?" Whether Christians admit it or not, disappointment with fellow believers can lead to disappointment with God.

Dismay with the Christian life also heads believers down the same path. If they faithfully pray for something they believe to be God's will but don't receive it, they may conclude that prayer doesn't work. This is a short step from the conclusion that God doesn't answer prayer. Disappointment with the Christian life also results in disappointment with God.

In 2 Timothy 1:8, Paul wrote to Timothy, "Do not be ashamed of the testimony of our Lord." There was the imminent danger that Timothy might become "ashamed" of Christ and the gospel, and Paul was trying to prevent that from happening.[3] For Timothy, the personal "suffering" (1:8), the opposition to his ministry (2:24–25), and the fact that God had not helped Paul out of his desperate situation (1:8) may have led Timothy to feel that God was letting him down. Paul was concerned that Timothy's attitude would lead to a cowardly spirit. Paul tried to encourage Timothy by assuring him that *he* was not ashamed of God in spite of his sufferings.

What this passage reveals is that it is possible for even Christian leaders like Timothy to become ashamed of God when He doesn't seem to be taking proper care of His servants or keeping His promises to them.

J. I. Packer acknowledged the possibility of true Christians feeling upset with God in his book *Hot Tub Religion:*

> Stop! Look! Listen! Here is a perfect instance of a kind of spiritual perplexity that (I dare to affirm) every child of God experiences sooner or later. Be warned: it can be appallingly painful, and if you are not prepared to meet it, it can embitter you, maim you emotionally and to a

great extent destroy you—which, be it said, is Satan's goal in it, every time. What happens is that you find yourself feeling that God plays cat and mouse with you. Having lifted you up by giving you hope, He now seems to throw you down by destroying it. What He gave you to lean on He suddenly takes away, and down you go.

But do not say that these things never happen to truly faithful folk; you know perfectly well they do. And when they do, the pain is increased by the feeling that God has turned against you, and is actively destroying the hopes that He Himself once gave you.[4]

FAMINE YEARS

Is it possible that a Christian, a true Christian, could stop living for the Lord for five years, ten years, twenty years, or even more because of disappointment?

In 1 Corinthians 3:1–3, the apostle Paul rebuked the Corinthian believers for living like spiritual babies instead of spiritual adults. This does not mean that the Corinthians were consciously sinning at every moment; this is not even true of unbelievers. In fact, Paul commended them for "holding firmly" to the basic doctrines of the Christian faith (1 Cor. 11:2); nevertheless, he was concerned about the gap between their spiritual age and Christian maturity.

If Christians are not consciously involved in the process of becoming holy and live for any significant length of time in a "fleshly" manner, it is entirely possible, if not likely, that they will appear to be "mere men" (1 Cor. 3:3). Discouraged and willfully sinning Christians will not completely stop living righteously, but the difference between them and unbelievers will not be that noticeable. The Bible does not reveal how long a true Christian can remain in a "fleshly" condition. The

Corinthian Christians had been believers for at least four or five years when Paul wrote his rebuke to them. Apparently, the only time limitation is God's patience.

Some object to the suggestion that Christians can continually sin on the basis of 1 John 3:9, which says, "No one who is born of God practices sin, because His seed abides in him, and he cannot sin, because he is born of God." John was apparently saying that true Christians will not consciously sin in a continuous and unbroken pattern, but what does this mean? How many times does a Christian have to commit a particular sin for it to be considered a "pattern"? Twice, three times, four, five, six? If the number is too low, no one could be a Christian. The fact is that the Bible does not give a number. God's Word simply indicates that genuine believers will not continue to consciously sin unabated.

Christians may struggle with certain sins over a number of years; however, true believers will sincerely acknowledge them and quit committing them for a while. Then they may slide back into them. In these real-life scenarios, the conscious sin is not truly continuous, but it is repetitive. Even the sin that's not repetitive may go unchecked for years if a believer is as deeply disappointed as Mrs. Hanover of Leslie Flynn's true story:

Roger Simms, hitchhiking his way home, would never forget the date—May 7. His heavy suitcase made Roger tired. He was anxious to take off his army uniform once and for all. Flashing the hitchhiking sign to the oncoming car, he lost hope when he saw it was a black, sleek, new Cadillac. To his surprise the car stopped. The passenger door opened. He ran toward the car, tossed his suitcase in the back, and thanked the handsome, well-dressed man as he slid into the front seat.

"Going home for keeps?"

"Sure am," Roger responded.

"Well, you're in luck if you're going to Chicago."

"Not quite that far. Do you live in Chicago?"

"I have a business there. My name is Hanover."

After talking about many things, Roger, a Christian, felt a compulsion to witness to this fiftyish, apparently successful businessman about Christ. But he kept putting it off, till he realized he was just thirty minutes from his home. It was now or never. So, Roger cleared his throat, "Mr. Hanover, I would like to talk to you about something very important." He then proceeded to explain the way of salvation, ultimately asking Mr. Hanover if he would like to receive Christ as his Savior. To Roger's astonishment the Cadillac pulled over to the side of the road. Roger thought he was going to be ejected from the car. But the businessman bowed his head and received Christ, then thanked Roger, "This is the greatest thing that has ever happened to me."

Five years went by, Roger married, had a two-year-old boy, and a business of his own. Packing his suitcase for a business trip to Chicago, he found the small, white business card Hanover had given him five years before.

In Chicago he looked up Hanover Enterprises. A receptionist told him it was impossible to see Mr. Hanover, but he could see Mrs. Hanover. A little confused as to what was going on, he was ushered into a lovely office and found himself facing a keen-eyed woman in her fifties. She extended her hand. "You knew my husband?"

Roger told how her husband had given him a ride when hitchhiking home after the war.

"Can you tell me when that was?"

"It was May 7, five years ago, the day I was discharged from the army."

"Anything special about that day?"

Roger hesitated. Should he mention giving his witness? Since he had come so far, he might as well take the plunge. "Mrs. Hanover, I explained the gospel. He pulled over to the side of the road and wept against the steering wheel. He gave his life to Christ that day." Explosive sobs shook her body. Getting a grip on herself, she sobbed, "I had prayed for my husband's salvation for years. I believed God would save him."

"And," said Roger, "Where is your husband, Mrs. Hanover?"

"He's dead," she wept, struggling with words. "He was in a car crash after he let you out of the car. He never got home. You see—I thought God had not kept His promise." Sobbing uncontrollably, she added, "I stopped living for God five years ago because I thought He had not kept His word![5]

This Christian woman admitted that because of disillusionment with God, she had "stopped living" for Him for five years. When we become disappointed with fellow Christians, the Christian life, or God Himself, our faith often falters. It's still there, but it can be extremely weak. In this weakened condition, we are very vulnerable to temptations from the world, the flesh, and the Devil. Normally we want to follow the leading of the Spirit and not sin, but doubts about God and His plan can often result in conscious sin until faith is restored.

How can we prevent disappointment and help others stay out of this predicament?

PART 2

WHY CHRISTIANS SIN—
THE LACK OF PROPER
DISCIPLESHIP

CHAPTER 5

THE NECESSITY OF DISCIPLESHIP

Keith Phillips, president of World Impact, a ministry to the ghettos and inner cities of America, began this ministry many years ago as a young man in the Watts section of Los Angeles. The ministry began with a bang but then almost died with a whimper because of discouragement:

I started Bible clubs in Watts. Scores of kid came. They all wanted to accept Jesus! And they all wanted to bring their friends. Mothers appreciated their kids getting religion, and teenagers were anxious to know when clubs would begin for them. Within a few years 300 Christian college volunteers joined me in teaching weekly Bible studies to hundreds of children. We organized evangelistic meetings. Many people attended—some just to see "those white folks." I would preach a simple salvation message, and invariably almost everyone would raise his hand to indicate a desire to have his sins forgiven and to be at peace with God. Meticulously we filled out decision cards and faithfully sent follow-up material to each new convert, not realizing that many of them were illiterate. I would pray with an addict or neglected child, say "God bless you," and then leave. Since I could not possibly shepherd all these new Christians, I reasoned that the Holy Spirit would take care of them. Hundreds of people in the Los Angeles ghetto "accepted Christ." My friends patted me on the back and assured me that I was doing a fine job. I wanted to believe them. And for a while, I did. But as the months blended into years, I had to admit that there was a serious problem. With all of these decisions for Christ there should have been changed lives—hundreds of them. But as hard as I looked, I could not find even one! Something had gone wrong. Partly because of pride, partly because of ignorance, I kept hoping that things would somehow right themselves. But I could not shake the gnawing feeling that everything had been in vain. There was no lasting fruit. The turnover rate in my Bible clubs was too great. Different youngsters came every week. Teenagers who had learned of Christ as children were still friendly, but they had become pimps, prostitutes or pushers. Former Bible club kids were running with street gangs. It seemed as if the gospel had not worked. I was discouraged. I almost quit. In desperation I went to God's Word. For the first time in my life I wanted to see what God said, rather than prove what I already knew. As I read Matthew 28:19–20, I received a startling revelation. Christ's commission to the church was not to "make converts," but to "make disciples." That was it! Even though I did not understand all the implications, I knew immediately that discipleship had been the missing ingredient in my ministry. I had hundreds of notches on my evangelistic belt, but I could not locate one maturing Christian. I had proclaimed the gospel, but I failed to make disciples. The more I studied the New Testament, the firmer my new conviction became. Discipleship is the only way to avoid malnourishment and weakness in the spiritual children for whom I am responsible. It is the only method which will produce mature Christians.[1]

There aren't mature Christians because many are consciously sinning as a result of disappointment with fellow Christians, the Christian life, or God Himself. Why? Because no one has ever properly discipled them.

Virtually all evangelical pastors, readers, and churches would say that they believe in discipleship. After all, the Bible mandates it (Matt.28:19–20), and Christ certainly modeled it. However, if the modern evangelical church is so committed to discipleship, why are committed Christians so few? Bill Hull, author of *The Disciple-Making Pastor*, said that "a generous estimate would find no more than 25 percent of evangelicals meeting Christ's standard for a disciple."[2]

Christian leaders and churches think they are doing discipleship, but in actuality they are not, at least not well. They spend one, two, or maybe three brief sessions with a new convert and then tell them to "come to church." As Robert Coleman stated:

With such haphazard follow-up of believers, it is no wonder that about half of those who make professions and join the church eventually fall away or lose the glow of a Christian experience, and fewer still grow in sufficient knowledge and grace to be of any real service to the Kingdom.[3]

In spite of the small number of Christians who ever really mature in the faith, evangelicals largely continue to believe that they are doing discipleship. How is it possible for them to keep kidding themselves?

WHY SOME MATURE

The answer is that some Christians still manage to grow and mature even though they are not being properly discipled. When it happens, evangelical leaders and churches can say to themselves, "The system really works, the people who are not growing are either unbelievers or slackers." Thus, the pleas of other Christians for biblical discipleship are dismissed and the status quo is maintained with the conviction that the problem is not primarily with what the churches are doing but with the people themselves.

Gordon MacDonald has publicly stated that he wonders what part human personality and temperament play in the process of spiritual growth. No one knows exactly, but they must play a part. Their contribution may explain why some disciples develop without disciplers.

I remember talking with a fellow pastor about how he matured as a Christian. He told me that no one took any interest in him after he became a Christian, and the church he attended gave him little or no teaching to grow on. Nevertheless, even as a new believer, he took it upon himself to do serious study of the Scripture and eventually to pursue formal theological education. For a long time he grew without anyone or any church really helping or encouraging him to grow. I know of many others like this man, and they all have a certain type of personality and temperament. They are often the kind of persons that go all out in whatever they do. They never do anything halfway. They are aggressive learners and doers. They are highly motivated to follow through and act on whatever they believe in. Often they are highly educated and like to learn. They are self-disciplined people who hang in there with tough tasks and keep going no matter what. In short, there are certain types of people who in a very real sense disciple themselves.

Of course, this is not ultimately to these people's credit. Apparently God has sovereignly provided certain people with the personality and temperament to disciple themselves with little or no human assistance. Perhaps this is God's way of ensuring sufficient leadership for His church at any given time regardless of the overall spiritual climate.

This is not to downplay the work of the Holy Spirit. Obviously, without His help and encouragement no one would ever grow as a Christian. Nor does this self-discipling of some deny that the majority of Christians require substantial human assistance in order to grow and mature as they ought. God's normal plan is for His Spirit to work along with human disciplemakers to develop His children, but God has apparently ordained that some will disciple themselves.

Several years ago I was instrumental in leading a man to the Lord who has grown in Christ at a phenomenal pace. Right after he was saved I met with him a few times for follow-up and he began attending the church I pastored. For a while I attributed his rapid growth to my occasional discipling efforts and my exposition of God's Word on Sundays, but afterwards I realized that I did not contribute that much to his maturing process. I'm not saying that I didn't contribute, but I am saying that my input was not as significant a factor in his growth as I initially thought. Until the last several years, the people who have grown significantly under my ministry have largely been "gung-ho" or self-disciplined personalities.

My experience has been repeated in other ministries. Some men and women are discipling themselves largely with God's help, but Christian pastors, leaders, and churches take too much of the credit for their maturity. At the same time, many Christians remain stagnant, immature, and disillusioned. Christian leaders blame these struggling believers for their situation when they are responsible for discipling them.

If some Christians are discipling themselves and the church is failing to help others, what's the problem?

FINDING A BALANCE

Much discipleship is unbalanced. Evangelicals either overemphasize knowledge or obedience. As Keith Phillips said, "One of the great tragedies of twentieth century Christianity is that many biblically knowledge-able believers are educated beyond their obedience."[4]

Many believers know far more about Scripture than they are practicing. Others are obeying what Scripture they know; yet they are still ignorant of important biblical principles and truths. An overemphasis on either knowledge or obedience can eventually lead to disappointment. If people do not know what God wants them to do, they will not be able to obey; if they do not obey, they will not know what God wants them to do. This mad circle can lead to severe disillusionment. Good disciplemakers emphasize both knowledge and obedience.

Imbalance also occurs because discipleship sometimes takes place only one way—en masse. Preaching sermons to large groups of people will not ensure that discipleship takes place. As Walt Hendrichsen said, "Disciples cannot be mass-produced."[5]

At the same time there are some who advocate personal, one-on-one discipleship to the virtual exclusion of small groups or corporate worship gatherings. This also is imbalance. Our Lord worked with individual disciples (John 6:5–7) but also with "the twelve" (Matt. 18:1) and "the seventy" (Luke 10:1). He also spoke to the masses.

Christians need a variety of people discipling them in a variety of settings. Otherwise, they miss out on certain truths and aspects of the Christian life and get too much of others.

Christopher Adsit, in his book *Personal Disciple-Making*, explained the importance of different discipling formats:

> The one-to-one dynamic will provide intimacy, where the disciple and I can get eyeball to eyeball on the individualized, personal, nitty-gritty issues that affect his life . . . there's nothing like the one-to-one tutoring/mentoring/apprenticing relationship to bring about accelerated growth rates.
>
> The small-group dynamic provides camaraderie, where the disciple can get into some give and take with people besides you. He gets to see that you aren't the only one who thinks as you do. Crosstraining occurs. He gets to be a "giver" instead of primarily a "taker." He rubs elbows with peers, encouraging and being encouraged.
>
> The large-group dynamic provides vision and momentum. He sees himself as part of an exciting, concerted movement. There's something about large group enthusiasm that's contagious. Often in these contexts our disciple's vision is lifted far beyond his little hamlet to the fields of the world, and a deep, lifetime commitment is made.[6]

ACCOUNTING STANDARDS

Not only is imbalance wrecking discipleship but also lack of accountability. Christians are afraid of accountability. Some of that fear is reasonable because accountability can be abused, but much of that fear is illegitimate and unfounded. Accountability to God and human leaders is thoroughly biblical (Heb. 13:17).

For Christians to grow and mature, they must be accountable for their time and behavior. Of course, this takes time and proper behavior on the part of Christian leaders, but it's worth it. As Chuck Swindoll said:

> Studies done in factories have proven that both quality and quantity of work increases when the employees know that they are being observed. If only God knows what I am doing, since I know He won't tell, I tend to make all kinds of excuses for myself. But if I must report to another or a group of others, I begin to monitor my behavior. If someone is keeping an eye on me, my behavior improves.[7]

Holding believers accountable for their growth (or lack of it) is difficult and time-consuming but absolutely necessary if proper discipleship is to take place, and proper discipleship is essential to the development of most Christians. Only a few can disciple themselves.

I'm not saying that discipleship guarantees that a Christian will never become disillusioned. Some Christians who become disappointed and consciously sin for significant periods of time were "properly" discipled. The reason that this happens is that no human discipler is perfect. We do not know with absolute certainty that those being discipled are truly "getting it all." Nor do we always disciple people correctly in every instance and in every way. We are human! What we need to remember is that even Christ, the master discipler, had one who didn't make it!

We must not be discouraged if some we attempt to disciple fall into conscious sin despite our best efforts. When we consciously sin we do so knowing full well that it is wrong, but we choose to do so anyway. We cannot and should not blame those who discipled us. Like the best of parents, the best disciplers are going to fail sometimes in some ways. This is no excuse for the sinner (Jer. 31:29–30).

Despite the occasional failures because of the human element, proper discipleship greatly reduces the possibility of disillusionment and tremendously increases the probability of continued spiritual growth. For many Christians, it makes all the difference between remaining immature and going on to maturity.

Chuck Colson, who knows what it means to be discipled, defined the task of all disciplemakers:

> Our task is not simply to get people to recite certain prayers so that we can move on to more fertile fields. We are to help lead them to Christ and then teach them spiritual disciplines and truths so that they truly can become disciples—followers of Christ, and in time teachers themselves. . . . When I asked Christ into my life, I had never heard of evangelical Christianity. . . . If there hadn't been someone to take me by the hand and walk me through the Scriptures, help me to pray, help me feel comfortable with others, I really wonder where I would be today.[8]

If discipleship is so important, what is the biblical model and method for discipling new believers?

CHAPTER 6

PRINCIPLES OF DISCIPLESHIP

Several years ago a young mother and wife apparently trusted Christ as her Savior through the witness of a friend. The person who led her to the Lord moved away shortly thereafter. Although this new Christian associated with other believers in her neighborhood and started to attend a solid, evangelical church, she was not personally and properly discipled.

As a result she did not grow very much as a Christian, and she struggled greatly with assurance of her salvation. She was on a constant spiritual roller-coaster ride; she even made a new profession of faith. A few weeks after her second salvation decision, my wife called her to discuss her decision to trust Christ again. It was evident to my wife that this woman had almost certainly been born again years before, but it was also clear that discipleship was desperately needed in her life. Through the course of the discipling process many questions about the Christian life were answered, and the basis for a growing relationship with God was firmly established. The spiritual outlook for this young mother is now much brighter.

Discipleship is vital to the spiritual growth of most believers. Without it many believers will not grow to spiritual maturity and many will instead become disillusioned with their faith. Everyone who is truly saved is willing to follow Christ and be His disciple at least at the very beginning of the Christian life. Some may still say that not all new believers are disciples and that many never were, nor ever will be, but God's Word indicates that in the early church every "believer" was considered a "disciple." These terms are interchangeable in the book of Acts.[1]

For example, in Acts 6:1–7, all believers in the fledgling church were clearly identified as "disciples" (vv. 1, 2, 7). The "congregation of the disciples" were clearly distinguished from "the Twelve" (v. 2). In God's eyes all Christians are disciples, and this was true from the very beginning of the church. Now this does not mean that every Christian will be a good disciple. As Charles Ryrie pointed out:

> If the examples of disciples in the Gospels may be carried over into today, then we would have to conclude that there will be some disciples who learn a little, some a lot, some who are totally committed, some who are not, some who are secret, some who are visible.[2]

Ryrie went on to offer as an example Joseph of Arimathea, who the apostle John said was a "secret disciple" (John 19:38; also see 12:42). Although all true Christians are disciples, Christians can be good disciples or poor disciples. What often makes the difference is proper discipleship.

1 Thessalonians 2:7–12 provides a good model of proper discipleship. In verse 7, Paul reminded the Thessaloni-

ans about how he had dealt with them as new believers. Paul said that he was like a "father" (v. 11) and a "nursing mother" (v. 7) to them. These two earthly pictures reveal some very specific discipling principles.

A MOTHER'S WORK

A Protection System

In verse 7 Paul said, "But we proved to be gentle among you, as a nursing mother tenderly cares for her own children." To *tenderly care* meant "to be as protective" as a mother bird is in covering her young.[3]

Gary Kuhne said in his book *The Dynamics of Personal Follow-Up,*

> A new Christian is more easily deceived by Satan than a more mature Christian. In fact, a new believer is more vulnerable in the fight against Satan's temptations than at any other time of his life . . . He needs the protection that a more mature believer can help to give him.[4]

We would not dream of leaving a newborn baby unguarded or unprotected for a minute, yet we often leave newborn Christians to fend off Satan and other dangers by themselves. They need protection all the time for a while!

A Love for All To See

Paul continued in 1 Thessalonians 2:8 to remind the Thessalonians of the "fond affection" displayed toward them and the fact that they "had become very dear" to Silas, Timothy, and him. The phrase *very dear* is a form of one of the Greek words for love—*agape*. Paul emphasized that love was expressed to the Thessalonians as new believers.

Love is crucial because it is the first of all the distinguishing marks of a Christian disciple. John 13:35 says, "By this all men will know that you are My disciples, if you have love for one another." From the very beginning of the discipleship process love should be demonstrated and emphasized because it is what being a disciple of Christ is all about. But love is also crucial because it is what allows disciplers to hold their disciples accountable. Without accountability the discipling process is almost worthless, and yet people are very reluctant to be held accountable. New believers may be willing to submit to God's authority, but submission to disciplemakers only comes when they see genuine love and concern in them.

A Shared Life

Also in 1 Thessalonians 2:8 Paul talked about the fact that the apostolic band had shared their "own lives." Initial discipling cannot be done from a safe distance. As Larry Crabb and Dan Allender stated, "Truth presented to people who are not involved in encouraging relationships will generally not realize its potential to change lives."[5]

Disciplers may not want to expose newborn Christians to all their personal flaws, but new believers need to see areas both of struggle and victory in the Christian life. LeRoy Eims related that "Dawson Trotman, founder of the Navigators, used to take a few of us aside and tell us about his defeats as well as his victories. But he was also careful to help us see that the mighty hand of God was always there to see us through."[6]

If new Christians only see the discipler's strengths, they can get discouraged by all their own weaknesses. At the same time, if they see only where a discipler fails, they're going to be disillusioned. Paul, while claiming to be the chiefest of sinners, tried to live "devoutly and uprightly and blamelessly" toward the believers (v. 10). He was their Christian model. It's one thing to tell new Christians what God expects and how they ought to act; it's another thing to actually show them what to do and how to do it. A demonstration of Christianity that comes from a shared life is very important in the process of discipleship.

A FATHER'S GIFTS

Exhortation

Paul switched to a paternal metaphor in verse 11 and discussed three other aspects of his discipling approach. First of all, he said that he discipled them by "exhorting" them "as a father would his own children." In other words he influenced them to adopt a suitable course of action.[7] It is not usually enough to simply be a friend to new Christians or to give them warm fuzzies. "Warm, affirming relationships that neglect the truth of biblical directives may promote happy feelings and improved self-images, but they do not promote godly character."[8]

Disciplers need to point out specifically what the Bible says the new believer should do and then influence them to do it. Example is important, but there has to be verbal exhortation to follow the directives of Scripture. Otherwise, the disciple might miss or misunderstand something important.

Encouragement

Once new Christians have been exhorted, they need to be encouraged. Paul said that he was encouraging them as a father would his own children. He inspired "them to continue in the desired course of action."[9] As important as it is to get disciples started in the right direction, it is just as important to keep them on the right track.

Everyone needs a pat on the back and a word of appreciation to keep going sometimes, but this is particularly true for those who have just started their walk with God.

I've heard it said that for every time a parent corrects a child, he or she should encourage them four times. I believe this is true, and I'm sorry to say as a parent I don't always follow through on this wise piece of advice. In many cases, parents encourage once for every four times they correct! Encouragement is not always easy, but it is essential to the proper development of children in both the physical and spiritual realms.

Insistence

Finally, Paul said that he was "imploring" them "as a father would his own children." An implorer testifies to the importance of a desired action and *insists* that the disciple does it.[10] Even with proper exhortation and encouragement, disciplers may have to be very firm with new Christians. This involves carefully explaining why following a certain biblical directive is essential and testifying to its importance. For instance, when new believers question the necessity of regularly reading God's Word, disciplers can explain from their own experiences the dire consequences for those who don't read the Bible and the abundant blessings for those who do.

Disciplers cannot force disciples to do what is right, but they can clearly explain what needs to be done and the results that will follow. If "imploring" new believers doesn't turn them around, they almost certainly will become discouraged with their faith.

A PARENT'S GOAL

The goal of discipling new Christians is given by Paul in verse 12: new believers walking "in a manner worthy of the God who calls [them] into His own kingdom and glory." The highest and best reason for growth and maturity is to glorify God with dedicated lives. Godly living brings praise to God. How do disciplemakers know when new Christians are properly and fully discipled so that they are living godly, and more importantly, will continue to do so?

Learning to Obey

In Matthew 28:19, after Christ commanded "make disciples" He went on to explain the process. The first step is "baptizing." The pattern of the early church as seen in the book of Acts was to baptize people as soon after conversion as possible.[11]

There are several purposes for water baptism, but one of the major ones is to get new Christians started as good disciples of Christ.

As Zane Hodges said:

It may be noted that from the beginning baptism was associated with the making of disciples. John noted that "the Pharisees had heard that Jesus made and baptized more disciples than John (although Jesus Himself did not baptize, but His disciples)" (John 4:1–2). Baptism may thus be properly seen as the first concrete step that a disciple takes in obedience to Christ.[12]

When a person trusts Christ as his Savior, he should immediately be given assurance from God's Word that he is saved, and then urged to follow through with baptism. New believers should be told that their willingness to be baptized indicates their willingness to obey and follow Christ. I have never had a new Christian refuse baptism when it was explained in this way.

True believers are indwelt and encouraged by the Holy Spirit to do what is right. Baptism may be strange or scary to new Christians, but if the discipler explains its importance and insists that it is necessary in order to obey Christ, new Christians will do it, and this establishes a strong precedent for obedience to Christ in their life, no matter what Christ may require in the future.

Learning to Apply

Once a new Christian has publicly identified with Christ in baptism and understands the importance of this step of obedience, then the second part of the discipleship process really begins, which is "teaching them to observe all" that Christ has commanded. They won't be doing it *all* right away. That will take a lifetime, but there are certain truths that disciples should not only know but be *observing*, that is, doing, before they are released from the initial phase of the discipling process.

The Bible does not give a specific list of things that new believers should know that indicate they are properly discipled, so no one can be dogmatic. I believe, however, that the list at least includes an understanding of assurance, sovereignty, God's promises, and God's will. The ones mentioned are definitely necessary because if they are not understood shortly after conversion, a new Christian can quickly become disappointed with God, the Christian life, or fellow believers.

In addition to knowing such truths, new Christians should understand the basic process of spiritual growth. They should be "observing" or consistently doing four things: reading the Word, praying, sharing their faith, and fellowshipping with other believers. It is not enough, however, for new Christians to simply be practicing these spiritual exercises. Believers are properly and initially discipled only when they start to enjoy doing these things. Before such a point of enjoyment, they may stop or become discouraged if the discipling is discontinued.

When young believers begin to enjoy spiritual exercises, they are getting to know God personally and experientially, and this is the ultimate goal of discipleship (John 17:3). Walking with God leads to knowing God. Obedience begets love, and love obedience. When young Christians experience the joy of knowing God personally, they are self-motivated and disciple themselves with the help of the Holy Spirit and the local body of believers.

Whether believers are discipled or disciple themselves, are there key truths that they should know at the start of their journey with God?

PART 3

WHY CHRISTIANS SIN— THE LACK OF BIBLICAL KNOWLEDGE

THE NEED TO KNOW GOD'S WORD

Two men were fishing one Sunday morning. Their consciences began to bother them because they were not in church. Finally, one fisherman said, "You know, I feel a bit guilty that we're not in church this morning."

"Well," replied the other, "if it's bothering you, why don't you say a prayer or something?"

The first angler answered, "Okay, I'll say the Lord's Prayer."

"Oh yeah? But you don't even know the words!"

"Want to bet I don't?"

"Sure do. Here's five bucks that you don't know the Lord's Prayer."

"Here's five bucks that I do!"

"You're on. Now let's hear it."

The first fisherman took a deep breath, closed his eyes and reverently intoned, "Now I lay me down . . ."

"Stop! Stop!" The second fisherman interrupted impatiently. "You don't have to finish. Here's my five. I didn't think you knew it!"[1]

This story may only be a fisherman's tale, but in reality there is a shocking amount of biblical ignorance today. In a nationwide survey of Americans, the Barna Research Group found that

- 58% do not know who preached the Sermon on the Mount.
- Most Americans cannot identify the names of the first four books of the New Testament.
- Half of all adults (52%) did not know that the book of Jonah is in the Bible.
- Half of all adults (48%) did not know that the book of Thomas is not in the Bible.
- Seven out of ten adults did not know that the expression "God helps those that help themselves" is not contained within the Bible.[2]

Clearly, the majority of Americans are very ignorant about the Bible. But evangelical Christians shouldn't feel too smug; we also lack sufficient knowledge of God's Word. Ignorance of God's Word is a major reason why Christians struggle with disappointment.

In his book *Hot Tub Religion*, J. I. Packer retold the story of the two disciples on the road to Emmaus (Luke 24:13–35). He correctly stated that the two were struggling with disappointment and unbelief in the wake of the crucifixion and an insufficient understanding of Scripture was a major factor. Packer said,

As ignorance of Scripture was the basic trouble on the Emmaus Road, so it often is with us. Christians who do not know their Bible get needlessly perplexed and hurt because they do not know how to make scriptural sense of what happens to them. These two disciples could not make sense of Jesus' cross. Many do not know their Bible well enough to make sense of their own cross. The result is a degree of bewilderment and consequent distress that might have been avoided.[3]

When believers get disappointed with God, fellow Christians, or the Christian life, they may have an insufficient knowledge of God's Word.

It seems very hard to believe that evangelical Christians could be ignorant about Scripture. After all, we have countless Bibles lying around our homes, ready access to Christian radio and television, piles of books giving us the biblical perspective on everything from acne to shooting zebras, numerous Bible conferences and seminars within easy driving distance, and large numbers of churches preaching the Word on a regular basis. Nevertheless, there is much we do not know.

Christians may be able to recite Bible verses from memory and tell Bible stories in exacting detail; yet we may not really understand God's principles and plan.

PRINCIPLES IN PRACTICE

Biblical stories were not included in Scripture simply to entertain or to provide opportunities for trivia questions. These narratives were given to convey timeless truths, to provide principles for life.

Jesus often used parables to illustrate truth, as in the story of the unjust steward (Luke 16:1–8). Sometimes Jesus and other Bible characters clearly stated the truths to be learned, but often a Bible reader has to intently study a story to understand its meaning. This is no easy task, nor is it a small or unimportant one. The Bible is primarily comprised of stories. But if "all Scripture is inspired by God and profitable for teaching, for reproof, for correction, [and] for training in righteousness" (2 Tim. 3:16), then discovering its principles is the task of every Christian. If Christians do not know the biblical principles taught by the Bible stories, they are missing out on a considerable amount of truth and are making themselves vulnerable to disappointment.

Believers fail to grasp not only biblical principles but also the "whole purpose of God" (Acts 20:27).

THE WHOLE STORY

Christians often spend time reading and studying portions of God's Word simply to meet current or felt needs. Psalm 23 is a favorite passage for those going through grief. But if Bible reading is limited to obtaining help for life's crises, believers will not know God's whole mind.

Sometimes believers look through the Bible to find verses about their favorite topics, but this also is an unbalanced approach. They can read all the verses on God's love and have a distorted view of God; He also hates some things (Heb. 1:9). Some might say that a greater understanding of God's person is more needed than a greater comprehension of God's Word, but this is faulty reasoning, as Harold Lindsell showed in a story given in chapel during my Bible college days.

Lindsell said that he was speaking to some Christian students about the importance of knowing God's Word. In the middle of his lecture a student stood up and said, "I don't think we need to waste all this time talking about the Bible. Let's just get to know God!" Dr. Lindsell did not rebuke him but simply asked how specifically the young man would propose to do it. The student thought for a while about the question and then sat down quietly. Lindsell then took the occasion to remind the students that one's understanding of God and relationship to Him begins with a serious study of the Bible.

Believers know God primarily through His revelation of Himself in His Word.

It is true that the Holy Spirit is teaching and leading believers into all truth (John 14:26; 16:13). However, the Spirit does this in conjunction with the written Word. If the Spirit alone was God's chosen method to reveal His truth, He would not have given the Scripture. For the Spirit's teaching ministry to be most effective in believers' lives, they must study and know God's Word. J. I. Packer's word of exhortation is appropriate:

> You can be quite certain that the Bible, God's handbook for living, has something to say about every life problem involving God's ways that we shall ever meet. So if you are hurting because of what you feel God has done to you, and you do not find Scripture speaking to your condition, it is not that the Bible now fails you but only that, like these disciples, you do not know it well enough.[4]

CHAPTER 7

UNDERSTANDING ASSURANCE

In the book *The Cult Explosion*, Dennis Adams, a former Jehovah's Witness, told why he became a born-again Christian. He said:

As a Jehovah's Witness, I was doing everything I possibly could to gain eternal life, and hoped I would have it someday, but I could never be sure.

In spite of my outward facade of confidence, which I always had at its best when talking with outsiders, I felt very insecure, and for good reason.

Many times these evangelicals would tell me, often with tears in their eyes, that they knew they had been born again, they had been saved from a life of sin, they had passed from death to life, that Christ had given them eternal life as a free gift, that they were His sheep and He would never let them perish . . . and they wanted me to open my heart to Christ so that I would have eternal life, too.

Of course I disagreed and argued, but deep in my

heart I longed to have the assurance they had. Well, praise God I have that assurance now![1]

WITNESS OF THE WORD

Like Dennis Adams, all people want assurance of eternal life. Of course, God is aware of this, and that is why He inspired the book of 1 John. This is clear from 1sJohn 5:13, which says, "These things I have written to you who believe in the name of the Son of God, in order that you may know that you have eternal life." God wants Christians to have what they also desire—assurance, but how can believers be sure they are truly saved?

John 5:24 is the record of what Jesus Christ had to say about this matter. There Christ stated unequivocally that "he who hears My word, and believes Him who sent Me, has eternal life, and does not come into judgment, but has passed out of death into life." The apostle John also plainly declared that "he who has the Son has the life" (1 John 5:12). God has promised that whoever "has the Son has the life." That's God's sacred promise.

When people put their trust in Christ as Savior, they may not feel any different; but they are, and they have to trust God's Word about the matter.

In *Windows on the Word*, Dennis J. DeHaan told about the importance of accepting God's Word about salvation:

> When George B. McClellan was commissioned Major General of the Army, he wrote his wife, "I don't feel any different than I did yesterday. Indeed, I have not yet put on my new uniform. I am sure that I am in command of the Union Army, however, because President Lincoln's order to that effect now lies before me."[2]

God's Word is the primary basis for our assurance, but it is not the *only* basis for assurance.

WITNESS OF LOVE

First John 3:14 says that "we know that we have passed out of death into life, because we love the brethren." There is no logical reason nor any basis in the context for limiting the "we" here to John and the other apostles. John was speaking of himself and his readers. In addition, there is no compelling reason to understand the phrase "passed out of death into life" any differently than in John 5:24. In both cases, John was referring to eternal life, as is clear from the context (1 John 3:15). John was saying that a further basis for our assurance is love for fellow Christians.

True Christians will not love all believers to the same extent nor at all times. What 1 John 3:14 indicates is that, whereas unsaved people once wanted little or nothing to do with born-again Christians, now they love them and want to be with them. That love will cross all boundaries, as the following indicates:

An American doctor traveling in Korea knew just enough of the language to get around. At a station stop an old Korean boarded the train and sat across from the doctor. He carried a large bundle in a white cloth. Soon the old Korean began to speak to the doctor, pouring out a torrent of words. The doctor replied with the only sentence he had memorized, "I do not understand Korean." The old man persisted. A second time the doctor gave his stock answer. This was repeated a third time.

In a stream of Korean words the doctor thought he had detected a somewhat familiar word. Had the old man said something about Jesus? His doubt vanished when the Korean pointed to the doctor and asked, "Yesu?

Yesu?" With a smile the doctor nodded agreement, "Yesu, Yesu."

Smiling from ear to ear, the Korean opened his large bundle and proudly displayed his Korean Bible. Then he put his finger on a verse. The doctor couldn't read it, of course, but carefully figuring out the approximate place in his own Bible, he read from 1 John 3:14: "We know thatwe have passed out of death into life, because we love the brethren." The barriers of language, culture, and age fell as unity of spirit flowed between the two men.[3]

A desire to be with folks of like faith is solid evidence that a person is a believer, but there is another piece of evidence that indicates one is truly saved.

WITNESS OF CHANGES

Second Corinthians 5:17 says that "if any man is in Christ, he is a new creature; the old things passed away; behold, new things have come."

This verse is not saying that Christians are totally changed in every way from how they were before they were "in Christ." The extent of these changes and the rate of change will vary based on a number of factors. However, if they find themselves thinking and acting differently in discernible ways after trusting Christ, this is significant evidence that they are truly born again.

The late Lee Atwater was once called the "pit bull of American politics." He was a man who went for the jugular vein if necessary to win a political campaign. However, several months before he died of cancer this man underwent a profound change of attitude and behavior. He began a process of apologizing to people he had hurt and offended over the past several years. He became a kind and gentle person. This dramatic turnaround was so sincere and genuine that even cynical, jaded media people had to admit that something real and wonderful had happened to this man. That something was someone, Jesus Christ. When people truly believe in Jesus Christ, they become "new creatures" and there will be noticeable changes.

Some may object to good works or changes in the lives of believers as a legitimate basis for assurance. They recognize correctly that there are times when good works and changes are not readily visible. The concern is that on these occasions the assurance of true Christians could be undermined. People who are genuinely saved could begin to question their salvation. This could be a problem, but it doesn't have to be.

People come to me for pastoral counseling, and often they are struggling with assurance. I explain to people again what it means to trust Christ as Savior and I ask if they are trusting Christ in this way. If the answer is affirmative, I ask them what if any changes have occurred. If they can testify unmistakably to the "fruit of the Spirit" being exhibited and to biblical changes in attitude and behavior, I assure them that they are saved, even if there is little fruit being exhibited at the current time. Apostates will no longer profess Christ as Savior and unbelievers will not be able to accurately testify to the "fruit of the Spirit" being displayed. Normally, I know people I'm counseling and can verify the presence of genuine fruit in their lives in the past. But I would not be afraid to give assurance to strangers if they professed Christ and could accurately describe the Spirit's work in their lives.

Of course, when I offer assurance to believers not living for the Lord, I also exhort them to start living as they should, which may involve getting properly discipled. Nevertheless, assurance should be based on both a profession of faith in Christ and testimony to the Spirit's work. Even if the Spirit's work is not discernible at certain times because believers are quenching the Spirit, assurance should be given if the Spirit's work has been evidenced in the past. Churches and Christian leaders need to systematically and regularly teach believers what their assurance is based on. If they do, even when believers sin or don't see fruit in their lives, they will still have assurance of salvation.

WITNESS OF THE SPIRIT

Now some may still object to any basis for assurance other than profession of faith in Christ and the promise of God's Word, but what about the inner witness of the Spirit? Romans 8:16 says that "the Spirit Himself bears witness" with the spirits of all Christians that they "are children of God." How does He do this? 1 John 3:24*b* says that believers "know . . . that He abides in [them], by the Spirit whom He has given." Two verses later, John apparently explained how believers know the Spirit is within them. He said in 1 John 4:2–3*a*, "By this [they] know the Spirit of God: Every spirit that confesses that Jesus Christ has come in the flesh is from God; and every spirit that does not confess Jesus is not from God." If believers keep getting an inner witness that Christ is God in the flesh, then they know the Spirit is within them. If they do not have this, then they need to examine themselves (2 Cor. 13:5); perhaps they really are not in Christ.

The Spirit definitely plays a part in giving Christians assurance of their salvation. If this seems too subjective for some Christians, they need to biblically reexamine how the Spirit bears witness. If they rely on their profession of faith in Christ, the confirmation of spiritual fruit, and the inner witness of the Spirit, they should not be troubled by doubts about their salvation.

EXAMINING THE WITNESSES

Some may agree that good works and changes in one's life are evidence of true conversion, but they may also argue that true assurance comes only subsequent to salvation when fruit has been properly displayed and assessed. In other words, brand-new Christians cannot (and, thus should not) be given assurance of salvation.

It is sometimes difficult to determine from a distance if there is genuine fruit in the lives of professing Christians. There are those who "sincerely believe they are saved but are utterly barren of any verifying fruit in their lives."[4] If this is the case, these individuals should not be offered assurance. Rather, that person needs to be lovingly confronted with the gospel again. However, we must be extremely careful about making judgments about specific individuals. True believers will be fruitful, but they are not always fruitful and may not be for indefinite and significant periods of time.

Also, believers may produce fruit that is not readily apparent. They may have certain thoughts, desires, and intentions that cannot be observed (1 Tim. 5:24–25).

IMPORTANCE OF WITNESSES

Rather than wait for fruit before offering verbal assurance to a new believer, it seems best to assume that those who clearly understood what they did in trusting Christ are truly born again and that the fruit will inevitably come, because the amount of fruit and the quality of that fruit depends to a great extent on assurance of salvation.

If new Christians are not given assurance of salvation solely on the basis of God's Word, then they are left open to the attacks of the world, the flesh, and, particularly, the Devil.

Some godly men are concerned about "evangelistic training seminars where counselors [are] taught to tell 'converts' that any doubt about their salvation is satanic and should be dismissed."[5] I also would be leery of dismissing *all* doubts as satanic. Nevertheless, Satan is a deceiver and an accuser (Rev. 12:9–10), and he tries to undermine the faith and assurance of newborn Christians.

Even apart from the damage Satan can inflict, a lack of assurance can still be an impediment to spiritual growth for new Christians. If new believers do not have assurance of salvation, the emotional upheaval can keep them from concentrating on growth and service and sometimes lead to frustration and doubt. Believers may become angry about not being able to ascertain for sure where they stand with God. Resignation to a state of spiritual limbo may result in conscious sin and ultimately disillusionment with their faith.

This does not mean that a Christian without assurance cannot possibly grow, but without assurance a Christian may grow slowly or not grow at all for a period of time. It is best to get new Christians off to a healthy start by assuring them from the beginning that they who have "the Son [have] the life." (1 John 5:12*a*) This is particularly true in the case of new Christians who have spent years hurting, struggling, and seeking for spiritual truth and reality. These folks need assurance from the very beginning.

During WW II, the Germans forced many twelve- and thirteen-year-old boys into the Junior Gestapo. These boys were treated very severely and given inhumane jobs to perform. When the war ended these boys wandered without food, shelter, or parents. As part of an aid program to post-war Germany, many of these boys were placed in tent cities. Here doctors and psychologists worked with these boys in an attempt to restore their mental and physical health.

One doctor had an idea and after feeding the boys a large meal, he put them to bed with a piece of bread in their hands which they were not allowed to eat. The boys slept soundly because after so many years of hunger they had a piece of bread in their hands and assurance of food in the morning.[6]

Just as assurance of food in the morning was crucial to the physical well-being of those boys, assurance of salvation is very important to the spiritual wellbeing and growth of most Christians, and especially for all new Christians.

CHAPTER 8

UNDERSTANDING SOVEREIGNTY

Not too long after I arrived in Iowa and settled into my second pastorate, a tragic accident shook our small town. A young man named Chris Seymour was driving home from a 4-H party early in the morning and lost control of his car. It struck a telephone pole and caught fire. The life of this seventeen-year-old boy was snuffed out almost instantly. This young man was an outstanding athlete, student, and person. The whole town was in a state of shock and mourning for some time afterward.

In a situation like this, people wonder why such tragedies occur. In their struggle to understand, they ask, "How was God involved?"

One of the local pastors in town, an evangelical, was asked by the newspaper to comment on the tragedy, and he replied that "it was just an accident and God had nothing to do with it."

OUT OF CONTROL

This pastor was expressing a theological perspective that is increasingly popular among Christians today. In his book, *God's Foreknowledge and Man's Free Will*, Richard Rice summarized this view by saying that "God maintains ultimate sovereignty over history. But he does not exercise absolute control."[1]

Many evangelical Christians don't feel comfortable with the idea expressed by Rabbi Kushner that "God would like people to get what they deserve in life, but He cannot always arrange it."[2] Even some non-Christians don't like this concept.

Elie Wiesel, a survivor of the Holocaust, said when he heard this: "If that's who God is, why doesn't He resign and let someone more competent take His place?"[3]

But more and more, there are Christians who are willing to accept the idea that God has in some cases relinquished control of the universe, and in times of human tragedy, this view is most readily embraced. The beauty of this concept is that it lets God off the hook. He is therefore not responsible for cars crashing into immovable objects and thus cannot be blamed or hated for the terrible things that happen.

COMPLETE CONTROL

Argument from Scripture

In contrast to this weak God view, the Bible teaches God's absolute control over the universe. In Daniel 4, God caused King Nebuchadnezzar, proud of his kingdom and accomplishments, to become like an animal in order to humble him (Dan. 4:32). As a result of God's judgment, Nebuchadnezzar did acknowledge God as sovereign and

gave wonderful words of testimony to this fact in Daniel
4:34b-35:

> For His dominion is an everlasting dominion,
> And His kingdom endures from generation to generation.
> And all the inhabitants of the earth are accounted
>   as nothing.
> But He does according to His will in the host of heaven
> And among the inhabitants of the earth;
> And no one can ward off His hand
> Or say to Him, 'What hast Thou done?

Argument from Meaning

The Scripture will simply not allow an understanding of God that denies that He is absolutely and completely in control of the universe. But, in addition to this,
there are other problems with the view that God is not
completely sovereign. One is that there is no real meaning in life's tragedies and therefore no lasting comfort.

After Chris's death, a number of well-meaning people
came to Chris's parents and told them that God either
had nothing to do with their son's death or that God
could not prevent it. This answer did not satisfy Carol
Seymour. If this was true, then her precious boy died
needlessly and without good reason. This total lack of
meaning in regard to her son's death was not acceptable
to Mrs. Seymour and she found no comfort in it. There
can be temporary comfort in believing God was not
involved in this kind of tragedy, but eventually the
thought of a meaningless death is much more disturbing.

Argument from Security

Even more distressing are the implications of a limited
God on the security of Christians. If Satan, nature, other
human beings, or some impersonal "force" is in control

at times, then Christians are in a very precarious position. They cannot, or at least should not, trust God for protection and safety. If God cannot or will not protect them and take care of them, then they better not leave the house in these perilous times, let alone fly on an airplane! God's sovereignty (or lack of it) has wide-ranging implications, as R. C. Sproul said:

> If there is one maverick molecule in the universe running around free of God's sovereignty, then there is no guarantee that any promise God has ever made will come to pass. That one molecule may be the very thing that disrupts God's eternal plan.[4]

Some time ago, Carol Seymour was given a tape of one of my sermons on the issue of tragedy. In it I explained that God is in control even when tragedies happen and that He allows these situations to occur. That does not always mean that in this life believers will understand why God allows certain things to happen. Yet they can trust that His reasons are always loving and wise from the perspective of eternity. People I respect and trust had assured me that Chris Seymour had put his trust in Christ as his Savior; and for the Christian, there truly is no such thing as an accident. Chris is with his Lord and although his family still misses him and always will, a person cannot be in a better situation than he is.

Recently, Carol Seymour sent me a letter. In it she says that "God's control of our lives is the only thing that makes any sense to me. . . . Life has become easier, in spite of the ache in my heart."

CONTROL AND CAUSES

The primary proof text for God's control of circumstances is often Ephesians 1:11, which says that God "works all things after the counsel of His will." This Bible verse is indeed indisputable evidence of God's absolute control over the events of this world. Everything that happens is ultimately according to God's plan. There are no exceptions. However, this verse does not say that God actually *causes* "all things after the counsel of His will." The word *works* does not necessarily indicate actual causation. This is the same word used by Paul in Philippians 2:13. It can mean to "work, produce, effect."[5] Any of these meanings would indicate that God is definitely involved in the process of making things work out according to His will. But none of these meanings specify how He is involved in the process. Sometimes God does cause things to happen so that His plan is done, but other times He simply allows things to happen that fit His perfect plan.

Romans 8:28 does not just say that God causes all things. It says that God causes all things *to work together for good.* The *good* result is Christians being "conformed to the image of His Son" (Rom. 8:29). This means that whatever happens to Christians will ultimately help toward that goal. This may involve God turning a seeming tragedy into something wonderful for His glory and man's benefit (John 9:1–3), or it may mean preventing a tragedy from ever happening. However God sees fit to do it, He is truly making everything work for the good of Christians and His glory.

If God actually causes all things to happen, He is responsible for sin, but the Bible says that God is holy (1 Pet. 1:16). This means that He cannot commit a sin. He cannot do anything that is contrary to His righteous character, nor does He cause or force anyone else to sin. (James 1:13). If God actually causes all things, He is the perpetrator of some very evil deeds.

In her book, *When It's Hard to Forgive*, Goldie Bristol told how her daughter Diane, a Christian, was brutally raped and murdered. Mrs. Bristol believed that her daughter's death was a part of God's loving, wise, and eternal plan, but she also said that she was sure that her "daughter's assailant and God had not planned together to attack her. But even though He had the power to, God did not step between them to stop the murder. The sole responsibility for Diane's death rests on the one who caused it."[6]

Now it is true that God's justice constrains Him to step into various situations and act in judgment, but human beings cannot know (most of the time) whether God's justice requires Him to take action or whether He is simply allowing something to happen as a part of His eternal plan. Nevertheless, God will never commit a sin and whatever happens to Christians is a part of a divine plan.

V. Gilbert Beers suffered the unexpected death of his son Doug. In his book, *Turn Your Hurts Into Healing*, Beers said,

> I found it immensely helpful to have settled certain things in my own mind before Doug's accident. I can't imagine the turmoil of mind if I had to sort out all of these things in the moments after the news came to me. I believe if you settle the following matters . . . in your more tranquil moments, instant tragedy will be less difficult to accept:
>   1. God is in control of His universe.
>   2. God does not direct every tragedy or accident.[7]

If Christians fail to acknowledge God's absolute control over their lives, they will be insecure. This can lead to disillusionment, and ultimately, conscious sin. If Christians attribute terrible sins to God, they can become angry and disappointed with God, which can also lead to willful sin. When they properly understand

God's absolute control over their lives, trusting Him will not be easy in the midst of suffering and tragedy, but it will bring more comfort because they know He is both loving and strong.

But how does God exercise His control over our lives? What has He promised to do and not promised to do? This is a vital issue in regard to significant spiritual growth and avoidance of sin.

CHAPTER 9

UNDERSTANDING GOD'S PROMISES

In the reading for 12 July 1989 of *Our Daily Bread*, the writer related the true story of a father whose son was a pilot during World War II. This father was confident that his son would return home safely from the war. The basis of his confidence was Psalm 91:7, which says, "A thousand may fall at your side, and ten thousand at your right hand; but it shall not approach you." This man understood this verse as a promise from God that his son would not be killed. He believed that God would protect his son no matter what. Yet the young man did die in battle, and apparently the news had a devastating effect on this father.

It is crucial that Christians have a good understanding of what God has promised, *and* what He has not promised. If believers do not have sufficient knowledge in these areas, they are very susceptible to disappointment. Unfortunately, this is exactly the situation today for many Christians. From personal ministry experience and private observations, I would have to agree with Philip Yancey, who said,

> I found that for many people there is a large gap between what they EXPECT from their Christian faith and what they actually experience. From a steady diet of books, sermons, and personal testimonies, all promising triumph and success, they learn to expect dramatic evidence of God working in their lives. If they do not see such evidence, they feel disappointment, betrayal and often guilt.[1]

Christians often have unrealistic and wrong expectations about the Christian life because they have erroneously claimed certain promises from Scripture. What are some of the promises that have been claimed and how have these passages been misunderstood?

OLD TESTAMENT PROMISES

There are Old Testament promises that were written to Old Testament saints, not to the church or New Testament believers. These passages do have application and profit for believers today, as does all Scripture (2 Tim. 3:16–17). These promises teach believers about how God has acted in history. They show how powerful He really is and that He is actively involved in the lives of believers. However, to apply these promises to Christians today is both erroneous and dangerous to their spiritual health. Some Old Testament promises apply generally to believers today, but not directly or completely. For instance, in Deuteronomy 28:2,15, Moses said,

> "and all these blessings shall come upon you and overtake you, if you will obey the LORD your God. . . . But it

shall come about, if you will not obey the LORD your God,
to observe to do all His commandments and His statutes
with which I charge you today, that all these curses shall
come upon you and overtake you.

This promise of either material blessing or cursing is
a part of God's treaty with the nation Israel (Deut. 29:1).
Christians today should not claim this passage as a
promise that God will increase the size of their families,
herds, and harvests if they obey Him (Deut. 28:11).

There is a general promise in this passage for New
Testament believers. If they disobey God they will reap
severe consequences; if they obey God they will reap
good consequences.(Gal. 6:7–9)

NEW TESTAMENT PROMISES

In determining whether or not an Old Testament
promise applies to believers today, Christians should see
if the promise is repeated in the New Testament, either
specifically or generally. The nation of Israel is not the
church, so promises given to Israel cannot always be
specifically applied to believers. Some would see the
church as a "spiritual" Israel, but this is highly debat-
able.[2]

The New Testament is God's final and ultimate Word
to the church. God's basic character has not changed, but
some of His specific methods of dealing with believers
have changed. Just as believers are no longer under Old
Testament law (Rom. 7:6) and only follow Old Testament
commandments that are repeated in the New Testament, they should not bank on any specific Old Testament promise unless it is specifially reconfirmed in the
New Testament. If they fail to understand or accept this,
disappointment with God may follow.

GENERAL PROMISES

In addition, some promises in Scripture are *generally*, but not *absolutely*, true. This is particularly and primarily the case with the promises that are proverbial. Proverbs 15:1 says that "a gentle answer turns away wrath," and this is almost always true; but most Christians have experienced at least one occasion where a gentle answer was met with angry words anyway. Christians must keep this in mind or risk disillusionment.

CONDITIONAL PROMISES

Furthermore, there are promises in Scripture that are contingent on certain *conditions* being met by the believer. A prime example is Psalm 84:11, which says, "No good thing does He withhold from those who walk uprightly." This is a promise that God will not withhold anything good from believers, but many Christians apparently either fail to notice or forget that it is conditioned upon righteous living. God often gives believers "good things" even when they are not living right because He is gracious. Sometimes believers may even accuse God of failing them when the the real problem is their own blindness to His blessings.

NO PROMISES AT ALL

Finally, some of the promises that Christians cling to are not really promises at all. Third John 2, for instance, is understood by some to be a promise that God always desires Christians to be healthy and wealthy. The verse reads, "I pray that in all respects you may prosper and be in good health, just as your soul prospers." However, this verse is not a blanket promise of health and wealth or an expression of God's will for believers in every situation. John is simply expressing *his* wish for a dear friend, which God may or may not have granted.

Believers must be careful about what they claim as a promise, because when these "promises" fail to materialize they can become very discouraged. Charles Sell related the following in his book *The House on the Rock*:

> In Beaver Valley, Pennsylvania, Bill and Linda Barnhart believed with all their heart that God would heal Justin, their two-year-old son, when he became ill. No doctors were called. Even when his stomach swelled, they continued to believe. After he was listless, pale, and looking like a starving child of a prison camp, they trusted. Eventually they called someone, a funeral director; he called the coroner. Justin's little abdomen contained a four-to-five pound tumor that had taken all his nourishment, literally starving him to death. The coroner called the police. Found guilty of involuntary manslaughter and endangering the welfare of a child, Bill was fined and sentenced to fifty-nine months probation.
>
> Later, Bill's brother, Bob, was answering a reporter who had asked why medical help was not summoned. He opened his Bible and told the reporter that James 5:16 promises God will save the sick; Jeremiah 46:11 reads: "In vain shalt thou use many medicines; for thou shalt not be cured." And then he said, "We feel that God wrote this Bible. Now how are you gonna walk up to the pearly gates when the time comes and say, 'God, You didn't mean Jeremiah 46:11. You didn't mean all these Scriptures.' If He didn't mean it, why did He put it in the Bible?"[3]

God does "mean" everything He says, but believers must determine whom He means it for and in what way He means it.

Many Christians today apparently believe that God has promised either that they won't suffer at all or won't suffer much if they live righteously. In Philippians 1:29, Paul said that "it has been granted for Christ's sake, not only to believe in Him, but also to suffer for His sake." Christians should not be surprised or disturbed by suffering because they "have been destined for this" (1 Thess. 3:3). John Wimber, founder of the Vineyard Movement, believes that it is often God's will to physically heal Christians today, but even he admits that "some type of suffering is a mark of the Christian life."[4]

Christians may suffer for Christ's sake (Col. 1:24) or to purify their lives (1 Peter 1:6–7). Sometimes God uses suffering to bring maturity (James 1:2–4) or to display a believer's righteousness, as in Job's case. Whatever the reason, suffering is a normal, inevitable part of the Christian life.

However, as Warren Wiersbe has said: "People live by promises, not explanations."[5] And God has promised other things besides suffering.

WONDERFUL PROMISES

Second Peter 1:4 says that God has given "precious and magnificent promises." Wesley once wrote that "I scarce remember to have opened the New Testament but upon some great and precious promise, and I saw more than ever that the Gospel is in truth one great promise."[6]

The Bible contains promises for both this life and the next. In Hebrews 13:5, God promises to never leave (either deliberately or accidentally) the believer; in Philippians 4:19 to meet needs through the riches of Christ; and in 1 Corinthians 10:13 to make a way of escape from temptation. These are all great promises for today, not just "pie in the sky."

But the Bible also promises "pie in the sky," and what a pie it is! In John 14:1–3, Christ guaranteed that there is a place for His followers in the Father's house. It is a wonderful place where there will no longer be any death or pain or emotional distress, just the blessing of being in the presence of God Himself (Rev. 21:3–4). Furthermore, Christians will make it there because the ultimate burden is on God, not them to "bring it to pass" (1 Thess. 5:24). Christ is coming again for both those Christians who have already died and for those believers who remain alive (1 Thess. 4:16–17).

These promises should be a tremendous encouragement to all Christians every day, and believers should not minimize or fail to appropriate God's promises. If they do, they may become disappointed with God.

Some Christians try to avoid disappointment by lowering their expectations of God. Delores Kuenning in her book *Helping People Through Grief* apparently adopted this approach. She said that Christians should accept the fact that "God has not promised us anything but to be with us and love us."[7] God has in fact promised considerably more. He has promised believers "abundant life" (John 10:10), but to have it, they must remember and appropriate God's wonderful promises.

There was a man named Steven Marsh, whose aunt willed him a family Bible and a few hundred dollars while he was still a relatively young man. He spent the money and threw the Bible in the attic without opening it. For thirty years he lived in virtual poverty until one day, as he prepared to move in with his son, he came across the Bible once again. He opened it and found scattered throughout its pages five thousand dollars in cash (and this was when the dollar was really worth something).[8] All through the past thirty years he had suffered needlessly. If he had simply opened that Bible and appropriated the money he could have lived much more comfortably.

God's spiritual riches must be appropriated. Understanding what God has and has not promised is essential for spiritual growth and victory over sin. But knowing and understanding God's will is equally important.

CHAPTER 10

UNDERSTANDING GOD'S WILL

In an article in Moody Monthly some time ago, I read about a Christian couple who felt the Lord was leading them to open a Christian bookstore in a small community as a ministry. A Christian businessman who owned several bookstores tried to discourage them because he believed that the community was too small to support it. This couple, however, believed that God would help them to overcome any obstacle because He had "called" them to that ministry. Apparently, they put a lot of money into the project, but a short time later the business went under and they "lost it all."[1]

When a situation like this occurs it is very sad. One hates to see another brother and sister in Christ involved in a financial disaster. But, beyond the monetary loss, there can be even a greater one: loss of trust in God. This couple, who so fervently believed that it was God's will for them to open a bookstore, could be deeply disappointed, which could lead to disillusionment with God. Why did God "lead" them into something that was going to be a complete failure? And if God wasn't leading them into the bookstore business, why didn't He make that clearer?

People have gone into marriages, business deals, and other assorted ventures because they felt they were "God's will." Then when things did not work out or totally collapsed, these people got very upset with God. They often felt that God had betrayed them. Certainly this was not the case, but what happened in these situations?

God does sometimes lead us into situations that could be considered "disasters" from a human perspective. God sent Ezekiel as a prophet to Israel and told him, "You shall speak My words to them whether they listen or not" (Ezek. 3:7). God knew Israel would not listen, and yet He sent Ezekiel to them anyway. God explained that at least "they will know that a prophet has been among them" (Ezek. 2:5). God's standard of success is not the same as the world's or even a Christian's (Isa. 55:8–9). What may appear to believers to be failure is not actually failure at all in God's eyes. Nevertheless, when things go completely sour, it is often because Christians do not understand how to correctly find God's will.

THE BIBLE AND GOD'S WILL

Many Christians acknowledge the sufficiency of God's Word in determining God's will. Wayne Grudem, in his book *The Gift of Prophecy*, defined the concept this way:

> The sufficiency of Scripture means that Scripture contains all the words of God which He intends His people to have at each stage of redemptive history, and that it contains everything we need God to tell us for salvation, for trusting Him perfectly and for obeying Him perfectly.[2]

Yet, even though many Christians agree that God's Word is sufficient for finding God's will, they still seem to miss His will too often. What is wrong? Many do not know God's Word nearly as well as they should. They need to be much more careful and thorough students of the Bible.[3]

COUNSELORS AND GOD'S WILL

They also need to be much more willing to seek counsel from more mature believers, those who have walked with God for a number of years and have sought to do His will. They should seek out people who can help fill in the blank spots in their understanding of God's Word, and who can also help them put the knowledge of God's Word into practice.

Proverbs 11:14 says that "where there is no guidance, the people fall, but in an abundance of counselors there is victory." This passage not only affirms the need for mature counsel in determining God's will but also the importance of seeking out more than one counselor. One person could steer another wrong, but several mature believers should not.

There is a spirit of independence in many believers today that is not biblical or healthy. Paul Little touched on this when he said,

I get very suspicious of people who come with very pious and spiritual language, telling me that God has led them to do some wild, outlandish thing, and nobody else has gotten the message. Undoubtedly, God may in rare instances guide us in a way that is totally contrary to the thinking of equally committed Christians, but I think it would be the rare exception rather than the rule.[4]

101

THE HOLY SPIRIT AND GOD'S WILL

Believers need to be more sensitive to and dependent upon the Holy Spirit. After all, the Holy Spirit is essential for understanding what God's Word says. It is the Spirit of God that ultimately teaches Christians what God is saying through Scripture (1 Cor. 2:12–13). It is also the Spirit who guides them into "all the truth" (John 16:13).

Now someone might say, "I'm carefully reading God's Word, relying on the counsel of others, and am sensitive to the Holy Spirit, but my life is still messed up!" Even if someone is doing these things, he or she may still have a faulty view of how to find and confirm God's will.

FEELINGS AND GOD'S WILL

One erroneous belief is that God reveals His will primarily through feelings or impressions given to the believer by the Holy Spirit. This is often referred to as the "still, small voice." Many Christians, while not denying the importance of Scripture, place more importance for direction on these impressions than on God's Word.

This is extremely dangerous. As John Wesley warned over 200 years ago, "Do not hastily ascribe things to God. Do not easily suppose dreams, voices, impressions, visions or revelations to be from God. They may be from Him. They may be from nature. They may be from the Devil."[5]

Instead, as Wayne Grudem said, "the focus of our search for God's will ought to be on Scripture, not primarily on seeking guidance through prayer for changed circumstances or altered feelings or direct guidance from the Holy Spirit apart from Scripture."[6]

The Bible indicates that we who are "sons of God" are definitely "being led by the Spirit of God" (Rom. 8:14). The Holy Spirit is continually leading believers away from sin and toward what is morally right. But how specifically does He do this? The Scripture does not explicitly tell us how the Spirit leads, but John 14:26 seems to indicate the normal procedure.

John 14:26 was a promise to the apostles that the Holy Spirit would help them to remember what Christ had taught and said. This would be crucial as they would have the major responsibility for putting Christ's life and teachings into writing. This verse is also for Christians today because the

> Holy Spirit comes to live with us and be in us (14:17), too; and He helps us to call to mind, as we need them, the words of Scripture we have first learned. This blessed promise should not prompt us to think that we need not bother to learn what Scripture teaches, for the Spirit can scarcely enable us to remember what we have never read or heard.[7]

The Spirit leads by teaching believers as they read God's Word and then reminding them what it says when they need it. When confronted by daily decisions and temptations, the Spirit brings to their remembrance the appropriate verses and biblical principles. Whether they follow His leading or not is another issue.

The Word of God is important in believers' lives, but does the Holy Spirit ever bring to our minds truth that is generally, but not specifically revealed in Scripture?

I think of a friend I met in seminary who was sitting at home in North Dakota one night watching television when he heard a "voice" telling him to "go to seminary." Now he was at the time a successful and established businessman with no prior desire to pursue full-time vocational ministry, although he was a godly man and active in his local church. A few minutes after this strange incident, his wife came into the room and informed him that she had just heard a "voice" telling her that they should "go to seminary." According to my friend, they could not account for this phenomena through purely natural explanations and so they decided to pursue seminary and pastoral ministry as a result. He and his wife are now actively involved in ministry and God is using them for His glory.

The leading of my friend by God's Spirit seems to be the exception, not the rule. God doesn't lead this way on a regular basis. Even those who emphasize the active work of the Spirit today recognize this is true. Donald Gee, a Pentecostal, said,

> An examination of the Scriptures will show us that as a matter of fact the early Christians did not continually receive such voices from heaven. In most cases they made decisions by the use of what we call "sanctified common sense" and lived quite normal lives. Many of our errors where spiritual gifts are concerned arise when we want the extraordinary and exceptional to be made the frequent and habitual. Let all who develop excessive desire for "messages" through the gifts take warning from the wreckage of past generations as well as of contemporaries.[8]

Although God may occasionally choose to lead through special guidance even today, believers should not expect it. Rather, they should view God's Word and the Spirit's normal method of leading as sufficient, unless God sovereignly decides to do something unusual.

Special guidance by the Spirit will never be contrary to God's Word, and it should be confirmed by mature believers who know God's Word well. Impressions or voices should never take priority over God's revealed will *or* mature, godly counsel based on God's Word.

Indeed, any inner message that tells believers what the future holds is to be rejected immediately. Consider the following incident from the life of Dr. James Dobson:

> Determining the will of God by means of feelings or impressions always reminds me of the exciting day I completed my formal education at the University of Southern California and was awarded a doctoral degree. My professors shook my hand and offered their congratulations, and I walked from the campus with the prize I had sought so diligently. On the way home in the car that day, I expressed my appreciation to God for His obvious blessing on my life, and I asked Him to use me in any way He chose. The presence of the Lord seemed very near as I communed with Him in that little red Volkswagen.
>
> Then, as I turned a corner (I remember the precise spot), I was seized by a strong impression which conveyed this unmistakable message: "You are going to lose someone very close to you within the next twelve months. A member of your immediate family will die, but when it happens, don't be dismayed. Just continue trusting and depending on Me."
>
> Since I had not been thinking about death or anything that would have explained the sudden appearance of this premonition, I was alarmed by the threatening thought. My heart thumped a little harder as I contemplated who might die and in what manner the end would come. Nevertheless, when I reached my home that night, I told no one about the experience.
>
> One month passed without tragedy or human loss. Two and three months sped by, and still the hand of death failed to visit my family. Finally, the anniversary

of my morbid impression came and went without consequence. It has now been more than a decade since that
frightening day in the Volkswagen, and there have been
no catastrophic events in either my family or among my
wife's closest relatives. The impression has proved
invalid.[9]

INNER PEACE AND GOD'S WILL

Another popular but erroneous belief about finding
and confirming God's will has to do with "inner peace." A
contemporary proverb says that "finding the plan of God
and conforming to it results in inner harmony. Missing it
inevitably produces 'inner discord.'"

A lack of inner peace may indicate that believers are
not doing what God wants them to do. When the apostle Paul came to Troas a "door was opened for [him] in
the Lord," but he "had no rest for [his] spirit," so he left
and went to Macedonia (2 Cor. 2:12–13). However, when
Paul finally arrived in Macedonia, he still "had no rest";
he was "afflicted on every side: conflicts without, fears
within" (2 Cor. 7:5).

Sometimes Christians do exactly what God wants
them to do but they still don't have inner peace. One
reason "some people experience a lack of peace [is]
immaturity."[10] Sometimes believers don't have peace
because their decisions, though correct, are going to be
painful for them and others. Sometimes God's will
means doing something they may not want to do or
doing something that may cause other people to get
upset. On these occasions, peace may not accompany
their decisions, even though they are doing God's will. In
such cases the believer must find support for being in
God's will from other sources than human emotion.

CIRCUMSTANCES AND GOD'S WILL

Many Christians view circumstances as a definitive sign of God's will. This is yet another erroneous belief in regard to discovering God's will. In 1 Corinthians 16:8–9, the apostle Paul told the Corinthians that he had decided to "remain in Ephesus until Pentecost; for a wide door for effective service [had] opened to [him], and there [were] many adversaries." In this situation, Paul decided that it was God's will for him to stay in Ephesus.

Many Christians read this passage and conclude that Paul's circumstances were the determining factor in his decision, but this is the wrong conclusion. The circumstances could be viewed either positively or negatively. Paul could have looked at the "wide door" and concluded that God wanted him to stay, or he could have looked at the "many adversaries" and decided that God wanted him to go. One cannot say that Paul always went through an "open door" because in at least one case he did not (2 Cor. 2:12–13). Paul's decision to stay was not ultimately based on the circumstances, but on other criteria.

When my wife and I bought our present house we encountered some difficulties in closing the sale and financing it. In the midst of these difficulties, well-meaning Christians read our circumstances two entirely different ways. Some believers told me that our problems in purchasing the home were a "sign that God did not want us to buy it." Other Christians told me that our problems indicated that God was testing our faith and that he wanted us to "hang in there" and buy the house. The circumstances could easily have been "read" either way. As Garry Friesen said, "Circumstances define the context of the decision and must be weighed by wisdom."[11] This wisdom comes from God's Word, mature counsel, and the leading of the Spirit. If believers make decisions based solely or ultimately on circumstances, they can be very disappointed.

FLEECES AND GOD'S WILL

There is the mistaken notion that God reveals or confirms His will through "fleeces." Some Christians look at Gideon's fleece as a model for finding God's will, but there are problems with using Gideon as an example for believers. First, Gideon's fleece "was really an expression of doubt and unbelief,"[12] not faith or trust in God. Judges 6 teaches that God is sometimes gracious to His servants who are struggling with doubt, but this passage should not be understood as an endorsement of "putting out a fleece." Second, there is an "absence of any teaching or example in the New Testament that even hints at such an approach to decision making."[13] If Christians expect to find God's will on a regular basis through a "fleece," they are going to be disillusioned.

DESIRE AND GOD'S WILL

Many Christians today mistakenly believe that God's will is exactly the opposite of whatever they personally desire.

I read recently about a survey conducted among a hundred young Christians. I was surprised, but not shocked, by the findings. Ninety-five out of the hundred believed that if they submitted to God's will, He would either send them someplace they do not want to go, or would make them marry someone they do not want to marry.[14] Some cherished beliefs apparently die hard.

God does care about believers' interests and desires. After all, He had a direct hand in who they are and what they like and don't like. He is responsible for sovereignly placing them in the families and situations in which they grew up. God has allowed them to develop certain interests and desires, and normally His will is in line with those interests and desires, as long as they are morally acceptable and God honoring, not sinful or fleshly desires.

God's will may not be what believers think is best for them. However, God knows them better than they know themselves. If His will appears to be different from their heart's desire, they must trust Him. He knows what will make them truly satisfied and fulfilled in the long run. So they must follow His will and not be disappointed if initially it appears to be different from what they think they want.

CERTAINTY AND GOD'S WILL

Even if I understand fully how God reveals his will, how can I know for certain that I'm in God's will? This is an important question, because if a Christian has consistent and persistent doubts about being in God's will, then that person will eventually become dissatisfied with God. The answer is: If Christians make decisions based on God's Word, mature counsel, and the leading of the Spirit, then whatever happens is God's will and they are in God's will. This is true whether one holds to the traditional view that God has one "perfect" will for the Christian in every situation, or that God has more than one possible will for the Christian in any given situation.

If some Christians believe that God has more than one will in any given situation, then they cannot possibly miss it if they simply follow God's Word, mature counsel, and the leading of the Spirit.

On the other hand, if others believe that God has one, perfect will and sincerely try to find God's will through

Scripture, mature counsel, and God's Spirit, they also will not miss it; and I am not alone in this belief. Walt Hendrichsen and Gayle Jackson discuss this issue in their book *Applying the Bible*:

> Many people fear that they have entered into God's permissive will or received God's second best because of some decision they have made. Yet nothing in Scripture indicates that anybody enters into God's permissive will except through a flagrant violation of His known will.[15]

In other words, if believers do what is right, God will see to it that they end up right where they should be. A biblical example of this truth can be seen in Ruth 1:19–2:3. Ruth returned with Naomi to Bethlehem from Moab after their husbands died. When they arrived, Ruth realized that it was her responsibility to try to provide for the two of them. So with Naomi's permission she set out to find a field to glean barley in. Of all the fields around Bethlehem, Ruth "happened to come to the portion of the field belonging to Boaz, who was of the family of Elimelech" (Ruth 2:3). There is no indication whatsoever in the text of special guidance. Ruth just did what was prudent and right, and she ended up in exactly the right place. Somehow God intervened so that Ruth ended up in the place He wanted her to be. This is where human activity meets God's sovereignty, and the result is God's will being done.

Larry Ward, president of Food for the Hungry, definitely believed it was God's will for him to go to Bangladesh in 1972, just shortly after that country came into existence. War had ravaged the land and millions of people were hungry and homeless. However, when he arrived in Dacca, the new capital, he didn't think that he knew anyone there, and he had no idea what he could do to help with such massive problems. So he just bowed his head and prayed. As he did, God's Spirit brought a name to his remembrance, a missionary he knew was working in Dacca. He contacted him and the missionary introduced Larry to his landlord, who had just been proclaimed the first president of Bangladesh. These two men sat down together and worked out a plan to airlift twenty million pounds of food to the starving people of Bangladesh.[16]

This is another example of human activity meshing perfectly with God's sovereignty and thus His will being accomplished.

God's will, promises, sovereignty, and assurance are all issues that affect the relationship of believers to God. Understanding what the Bible has to say about these areas will start believers on the right road; but it is a long journey, and spiritual exercise will give them the strength to keep going.

PART 4

WHY CHRISTIANS SIN— THE LACK OF SPIRITUAL EXERCISE

THE NEED FOR
SPIRITUAL EXERCISE

B elieve it or not, according to John Naisbitt, "at least 100 million Americans, almost half of the population, are now exercising in some way, up from about one-quarter of the population in 1960. That is a 100 percent increase in regular exercisers. One in seven Americans now jogs on a regular basis."[1]

It is hard to believe that almost half of all Americans now exercise in some way on a regular basis. But whether this is precisely true or not, the fact remains that many Americans finally understand that physical exercise is often vital to a long life, and more importantly, to a healthy and enjoyable life as long as one does live.

What's more, Americans are beginning to recognize that sporadic or occasional exercise simply does not do that much good. If they are going to get some measurable benefit from physical exercise, they have to work out on some kind of a regular basis.

One basic reason Christians become disappointed with their faith and then willfully sin is a lack of biblical knowledge. However, a second and equally important reason is lack of spiritual exercise. Biblical knowledge and spiritual exercise are both essential to proper discipleship.

A. W. Tozer said in his book, *The Pursuit of God*, "the idea of cultivation and exercise, so dear to the saints of old, has now no place in our total religious picture." He preceded this statement by saying, "failure to see this is the cause of a serious breakdown in modern evangelicalism."[2] Tozer wrote these words many, many years ago. Although some Christians are beginning to realize the need for regular spiritual exercise, the situation is no better, and perhaps worse, than in Tozer's day. There is a physical exercise boom underway in this country, but spiritual exercise has not gained the same popularity.

First Timothy 4:7 says, "discipline yourself for the purpose of godliness." The word *discipline* here means to "exercise" or to "train."[3] This word often refers to physical exercise, but here it refers to spiritual exercise, which, in the context, includes the reading of God's Word (1 Tim. 4:6). There are other spiritual exercises as well, such as prayer, witnessing, and fellowshipping with other believers.

SPIRITUAL EXERCISE AND UNCONSCIOUS SIN

Failure to discipline themselves to do spiritual exercise is often an unconscious sin for Christians today. This failure is clearly a sin because "discipline" here is a command. God commands believers to do it, and they know they should do it. However, they often commit this sin unknowingly for two basic reasons.

First, the Bible is not explicit about how often spiritual exercise should take place. There is no verse, for instance, that tells exactly how often to pray, or for how long. Therefore, Christians can pray once a day or even once a week, and when the Spirit prompts them to do more, they can dismiss the prompting as an overly-sensitive conscience.

Second, in many evangelical churches, Christians can look around at fellow believers and see very little activity in regard to spiritual exercise. This indicates to them that they are normal and confirms their conviction that they are not sinning. Many Christians view the few who are regularly engaging in spiritual exercises as abnormal or "super Christians." These folks are viewed as people who are in a sense doing "extra credit" work.

Regular spiritual exercise is often viewed as admirable but not really necessary for a "normal" or fulfilling Christian life.

So the sin of not doing spiritual exercise is often an unconscious sin, but this certainly does not excuse it, nor does it make it any less serious. Failure to do spiritual exercises often destroys spiritual health.

SPIRITUAL EXERCISE AND GOD'S BLESSING

For instance, when believers fail to read God's Word as often as they should, they lose the blessing of having the God of the universe speak to them with encouragement, comfort, challenge, and wisdom. The Spirit uses God's words to lead and help them, so whenever they fail to read the Bible they limit what the Spirit can effectively do in their lives.

To a great extent, God's blessings are tied to involvement in spiritual exercise. Some years ago a bridge was built over a great river in one of the western states. It was decided that once it was officially open to the public, a $1,000 prize, along with several other gifts, would be given to the 100th car to drive across the new span.

A crowd had gathered, and excitement was high. At last, the car that would be number 100 was seen in the distance. The crowd began to cheer as the car approached the other end of the bridge. But then something happened. The car came to a halt, paused a moment, and then made a U-turn in the middle of the road. It began heading back in the other direction.

A police car raced after the car. Once apprehended, the driver was asked why he turned around. "Oh," said he, "when I saw the sign about a $1.00 toll, I decided I didn't want to pay the price."[4]

There is a price to be paid for spiritual exercise; it is hard work. No pain, no gain. Compared with the blessings that will follow, the price is not at all high, and every believer should be willing to pay it.

SPIRITUAL EXERCISE AND DISCIPLINE

Besides missing out on God's blessings, there can be another severe consequence of believers' failing to "discipline" themselves to do spiritual exercise. God disciplines them. As Hebrews 12:5 says, "those whom the Lord loves He disciplines." When He does this, Christians who have been sinning unconsciously may wake up and realize their error. On the other hard, they may not recognize their sin and wonder why God is being so unfair. If this feeling continues, it can lead them from unconscious sin into deliberate and willful sin. This is why new believers should do spiritual exercises from the very beginning of the Christian life, regularly and often.

Now someone may ask, "How much and how often?" God doesn't make hard and fast rules about this, but

God's Word gives two general principles in answer to this question.

SPIRITUAL EXERCISE AND GODLINESS

First, believers should examine their progress toward "godliness," which is the expressed goal of spiritual exercise (1 Tim. 4:7). *Godliness* is the fear or reverence for God that manifests itself in devotion to Him.[5]

If they are reading the Word, praying, witnessing, and fellowshipping to the proper extent, then their respect and awe of God will be increasing. They should find themselves more amazed by the display of God's power, more captivated by the beauty of His creation, and more ashamed of their sinfulness in light of His perfect holiness. Their love and adoration for God should also be growing. They should be more devoted to Him as they see His faithfulness, more grateful as they experience His infinite grace, and more in love with Him each day as they recognize His mercies. If their respect and love for God is not increasing, they are not disciplined enough.

The purpose of spiritual exercise is not just to serve God and to accomplish much for His glory, as important as that is. It is certainly not to simply keep believers busy. Activity is not the ultimate goal, but rather the development of a relationship with Him. This is what the Christian life is all about. Christianity is a personal relationship with the God of the Universe through trust in Christ and the work of the Spirit. This is why "bodily discipline is only of little profit, but godliness is profitable for all things, since it holds promise for the present life and also for the life to come" (1 Tim. 4:8).

Spiritual exercise builds up a believer's relationship with God. That is beneficial now and in the future existence with Him. Christians who desire to be godly and know God intimately must regularly "work out."

SPIRITUAL EXERCISE AND ENJOYMENT

Besides gauging progress toward godliness through spiritual exercise, believers should also measure their enjoyment of it. The psalmist says, "I shall delight in Thy statutes; I shall not forget Thy word" (Ps. 119:16). The word *delight* is used nine times in Psalm 119 in connection with God's Word. The psalmist took real pleasure in reading and studying God's Word. Spiritual exercise, like physical exercise, can be quite taxing and not always that enjoyable at first. But if believers discipline themselves to do it anyway, eventually spiritual exercise can be enjoyable. If it is and it is leading to godliness, then they know that they are working out properly.

Physical exercise lowers heart rate and builds muscle tone, but spiritual exercise leads to godliness and joy. Spiritual fitness is within the reach of all believers if they work out properly, but what are the right exercises?

CHAPTER 11

READING GOD'S WORD

Many years ago in a Moscow theater, matinee idol Alexander Rostovzev was converted while playing the role of Jesus in a sacrilegious play entitled *Christ in a Tuxedo*. He was supposed to read two verses from the Sermon on the Mount, remove his gown, and cry out, "Give me my tuxedo and top hat!" But as he read the words, "Blessed are the poor in spirit, for theirs is the kingdom of heaven. Blessed are they that mourn, for they shall be comforted," he began to tremble. Instead of following the script, he kept reading from Matthew 5, ignoring the coughs, calls, and foot-stamping of his fellow actors. Finally, recalling a verse he had learned in his childhood in a Russian Orthodox church, he cried, "Lord, remember me when Thou comest into Thy kingdom!" (Luke 23:42). Before the curtain could be lowered, Rostovzev had trusted Jesus Christ as his personal Savior.[1]

The supernatural power of God's Word can change lives, but people must hear it or read it for its power to be unleashed (Romans 10:17).

According to the Gallup pollsters, eighty-nine percent of Americans don't read the Bible daily. George Gallup said that "our frequency of Bible reading has remained virtually unchanged over the years . . . People revere the Bible, but they don't read it—that's what it comes down to."[2]

Some might say that although eighty-nine percent of Americans don't read the Bible daily, that figure certainly does not apply to born-again Christians. No one knows exactly how many Christians read their Bible daily except God, but my ministry experience indicates to me that the percentage of Christians reading the Bible daily is not that much higher than the general public. Christians realize that they ought to read their Bibles, and they do. However, the majority of Christians do not read their Bibles very often or often enough to really make a significant difference in their lives. Why? Perhaps they have not approached their reading in the right way with the proper attitude.

READ SLOWLY AND CAREFULLY

The psalmist said, "Open my eyes, that I may behold wonderful things from Thy law" (Psalm 119:18). Christians should always ask God To "open their eyes," to see spiritual reality, things unseen (Num. 22:31). God and the Holy Spirit want to do this for believers, but many Christians still complain that they are not "getting anything" out of God's Word, as the following story indicates:

A Christian couple in Georgia had always read the Bible every day. Yet they seemed to get little out of it and were usually relieved when their devotional time was over. They noticed, however, that it was quite different with Mandy, their 75-year-old cook and housekeeper. Whenever she picked up her Bible, her face seemed to light up with joy and expectancy. One day the man asked, "Mandy, how come you get so much out of the Bible? We read it too, but you seem to find things we never see." Mandy replied, "Well, I have to admit that I'm not educated like you and your wife. So I have to study it slowly, spelling out each word and praying as I go. You folks can skim over it fast, but maybe it doesn't sink in as good that way." The couple saw the point. Now they too go slowly and pray as they try to understand the Word and its practical applications.[3]

READ FOR THE EXTRAORDINARY

In addition to not reading God's Word slowly and prayerfully, many believers read only a predetermined amount of Scripture. They may decide to read two verses or two chapters, but then they quit whether they have received something "wonderful" out of the text or not. The word *wonderful* from Psalm 119:18 means "extraordinary." When Christians read the Bible they need to see the extraordinary—God's character and promises.

In order to do this, Christians must be willing to keep reading God's Word until they grasp hold of an important spiritual truth that God can use in their lives. This may mean that they read two or three times as much Scripture as they intended to on a particular occasion. But what is the use of reading a passage of Scripture just so they can say they've had their "quiet time" or done their "duty" for the day? They need to read God's Word until they see what God intends for them to see. If they don't, eventually they will lose interest in Bible reading.

The problem is not always too little reading but too little understanding and application. Psalm 119:15 says,

"I will meditate on Thy precepts, and regard Thy ways."
Some Christians may shy away from, or refuse to be
involved in, any form of meditation because of current
abuses and misuses of the practice. Unbiblical meditation is mental visualization in an attempt to create one's
own "reality."

Biblical meditation, in contrast, is the contemplation
of what God says is "reality" in order to better understand and apply it to our lives. The psalmist compared
this practice to the savoring of honey in the mouth (Ps.
119:103). Meditation on God's Word means rolling it over
again and again in the mind, contemplating its meaning and thinking about its practical implications. Psalm
119 implies its importance by explicitly referring to it
eight times, and it is often referred to and advocated
elsewhere in Scripture.[4] What's more, the practice of
meditating on Scripture has been shown to make a difference in lives of believers.

Dr. Paul Meier, a Christian psychiatrist, did extensive
testing of the spiritual and mental health of students
from an evangelical seminary several years ago. As he
told it:

> When the results came in, initially I was surprised and
> disappointed. Those seminary students who had been
> Christians for many years were only slightly healthier
> and happier than those who had accepted Christ in the
> past one or two years. The difference was not even sta-
> tistically significant. However, my disappointment
> turned to joy. I learned one of the most valuable lessons
> of my life when I found the factor that made the differ-
> ence. That factor was Scriptural meditation. Students
> who practiced almost daily Scripture meditation for
> three years or longer were significantly healthier and
> happier than students who did not meditate on Scripture
> daily.[5]

Christians need to first read the Bible and then take some time to meditate on its meaning and application for them personally. This is often crucial in getting something "wonderful" out of God's Word.

READ TO APPLY

Careful reading and meditation is only part of the task. Christians must apply God's Word. "But prove yourselves doers of the word, and not merely hearers who delude themselves" (James 1:22). In James' day, there was a debate among the Jews about how the value and blessing of God's Word was received. Some Jewish scholars believed that if one merely heard the Scripture it would automatically benefit the hearer.[6] However, James says that if Christians believe this, they are kidding themselves. In order for God's Word to be most effective in their lives, they have to personally apply it and act upon it. What's more, this is something they should do immediately after hearing God's Word. James explains why: "For if anyone is a hearer of the word and not a doer, he is like a man who looks at his natural face in a mirror; for once he has looked at himself and gone away, he has immediately forgotten what kind of person he was" (James 1:23–24).

The danger of simply reading God's Word and interpreting it without immediately applying it is that believers may not get the opportunity to do it later. Within moments they can forget what they saw in the mirror of God's Word before it has had a chance to affect their lives.

Dr. Howard Hendricks, a professor of mine at Dallas Seminary, used to say, "Interpretation without application is abortion." That's not just a pithy saying; that's what God's Word says. Readers of the Word should be appliers of the Word.

This is not to deny that there is a certain amount of value in simply reading the Word, even if believers don't remember it or consciously apply what they have read. To use an old but relevant illustration, it's like pouring water through a sieve. When you are done, there's not much water in the sieve, but at least you have a clean sieve! Simply reading God's Word does have a certain cleansing effect. What's more, the Holy Spirit can bring to remembrance portions of God's Word that have been read but have not been considered for some time (John 14:26). Nevertheless, the point of James 1:22–24 is that Christians should be striving for immediate application of Scripture.

Even if believers are getting some "wonderful" things out of God's Word, they may not be getting enough to keep them spiritually healthy. First Timothy 4:6 indicates that it is important for believers to be "constantly nourished on the words of the faith." The word *nourish* pictures God's Word as spiritual food. In order for Christians to grow they must be partaking of Scripture.

Many believers eat too much spiritual "junk food." Many Christians depend upon sermons, Christian books, even Christian romance novels, for their spiritual nourishment.

Several years ago the manager of a Christian bookstore in Des Moines, Iowa, said that Christian romance novels are "the largest-moving item in the store. Even though we're a Christian bookstore, the Bible is not the best seller here."[7]

There may be some spiritual food in at least some of these things, but none of these is an adequate substitute for reading in God's Word. Many Christians consume enough of God's Word to sustain spiritual life but not enough to produce significant spiritual growth. If Christians are not growing or growing very slowly, they are probably not consuming enough of God's Word. Christians should commit themselves to reading the Bible at least once a day, no matter what.

I usually recommend that a person read the Bible in association with something that is done without fail every day. It may be getting up in the morning, going to sleep at night, going to work, eating a meal, or taking a work break. But whatever the time or activity, it is crucial that Christians be "nourished" in God's Word every day. This is particularly true for new Christians or believers who have not arrived at the point where they actually enjoy reading the Scriptures. Christians should get to the point where they enjoy reading the Bible; it should not remain a duty or just an exercise indefinitely.

In order to achieve enjoyment, Christians need to continue growing in their ability to understand and apply Scripture. This does not mean that every Christian can (or should) be able to read Hebrew and Greek. Nor does it mean that every Christian should go to seminary. However, every believer needs to become a serious student of the Bible, able to handle "accurately the word of truth" (2 Tim. 2:15).

Many Christians continue to read or study the Bible the same way as when they first became Christians. They do not progress on to new methods and new Bible study tools. This can cause one to stagnate and lose the joy of discovery in reading the Word.

Some Christians say that God's Word is alive or "living" (Heb. 4:12), so every time they read a particular verse or passage, they will come away with a fresh insight. God's Word is "living," which means that it is always true and always relevant, but the ability to glean fresh insights from it is often directly proportionate to the ability to dig deeper into it. If Christians continue to read and study the Bible the way they always have, they may find that, even though the Bible is "living," they are getting less and less out of it.

There is a story told about a small New England town that desperately needed water. After workers had drilled 800 feet deep, they still had no success. About to abandon the search, the town officials consulted the U.S. Geological Survey. Their engineers examined the strata and decided that there was water deeper down. So they gave instructions to continue boring. When the workmen reached a depth of approximately 1100 feet, they finally struck water. Always before, the town had had to buy water from another municipality. Now that they had their own ample supply, this was no longer necessary. They also became the supplier of water to other towns.[8]

Every true believer begins the Christian life with a desire to read God's Word. However, if the Christian does not find "wonderful things" in the Word or enjoy reading the Word, that person can become frustrated. This can in turn lead to discontentment and willful sin.

In order to halt or reverse this process, Christians need to read God's Word carefully and prayerfully, meditate on its meaning, and then apply it immediately if possible. What's more, believers need to continually progress in their ability to dig deeper into the Bible.

Of course, reading God's Word allows God to talk to us, but we also need to talk to Him.

CHAPTER 12

PRAYING TO HIM

A tale is told about a small town that had historically been "dry," but then a local businessman decided to build a tavern. A group of Christians from a local church were concerned and planned an all-night prayer meeting to ask God to intervene. It just so happened that shortly thereafter lightning struck the bar and it burned to the ground. The owner of the bar sued the church, claiming that the prayers of the congregation were responsible, but the church hired a lawyer to argue in court that they were not responsible. The presiding judge, after his initial review of the case, stated that "no matter how this case comes out, one thing is clear. The tavern owner believes in prayer and the Christians do not."[1]

Most Christians say that prayer is very important and that they believe it makes a difference. Nevertheless, most Christians would have to admit that they do not pray very much or nearly as much as they should. As Gordon MacDonald put it, "No one would deny that prayer is important, but few believe their prayer life to be adequately developing."[2]

129

I believe that there is a reason for this. Christians do not really believe that prayer is that effective. They don't completely deny what the Bible says (James 5:16), yet their experience seems to tell them that God doesn't answer prayers very often. In fact, many Christians are surprised, sometimes shocked, when God does answer their prayers (see Acts 12:3–17).

Why aren't Christians more confident about prayer and God's willingness to answer prayer?

Some would say that the major problem is a lack of faith. The Bible says that God does not give answers to those who doubt or lack sufficient faith (James 1:6–7). The Bible also says that "if you have faith as a mustard seed, you shall say to this mountain, 'Move from here to there,' and it shall move; and nothing shall be impossible to you" (Matt. 17:20). Surely even the average Christian has faith "as a mustard seed." Thus, this is probably not the problem in most cases.

Some might say that Christians are just not praying according to God's will (1 John 5:14). However, it seems like many prayers that are offered according to God's revealed will are still not answered. I know a number of people in my church who have been praying for the salvation of their loved ones, and have been doing so for some time, but apparently to no avail. Certainly, these prayers are in accordance with God's will to a significant degree (2 Pet. 3:9). I don't believe that prayers offered out of God's will are a major problem either.

BE SPECIFIC

The biggest reason why Christians don't see God answering their prayers is because they don't pray specifically enough. Oftentimes when they pray for missions, they pray vaguely, "Please God, bless the missionaries all over the world." If they pray for a specific missionary, they don't mention a specific need.

I'm not quite sure why Christians do this. Sometimes the problem is lack of knowledge. They don't know exactly what to ask God for. However, in many cases I think they're afraid to step out by faith and ask God for something specific, because if they don't get it, then they're embarrassed or disappointed. The greater problem with vague or general requests is that God's Word specifically says, "You do not have because you do not ask" (James 4:2). God is a loving, heavenly Father, who graciously gives good gifts to both the righteous and the unrighteous (Matt. 5:45) and meets many needs without us even having to ask (Phil. 4:19). But there are apparently certain things that God would like to give us and are good for us that He won't bestow them on us until we specifically ask for them.

God undoubtedly has many good reasons for operating in this way. One reason may be that there is no way to recognize the answers to general prayers. Who knows how many times believers have prayed generally, and God has answered specifically? When believers pray specifically, they receive answers from God and recognize them as such.

I meet regularly with small groups of men. We meet for Bible study and extended periods of sharing and prayer. We are continually amazed at how God answers the majority of our prayers in an affirmative way. I'm sure that there is more than one reason for this, but I believe the crucial one is that we insist that all prayers be specific.

We not only tell God exactly what we desire, but we also usually indicate a certain desired time frame for the answer as well. God has definitely said "no" to some of our requests. But at least we know because we have prayed specifically. God has also answered requests much later than we desired, yet at least when the answers arrived we were able to recognize them.

When one of our current pastors was asked to come and join our church staff he shared with the congregation how he had prayed specifically about the ministry God would have for him. He and his family came up with twenty-one specific requests regarding their future ministry. All twenty-one of their requests were answered by the time they arrived at our church!

When Christians pray specifically, God in His infinite wisdom and love may not grant their request and they may be momentarily disappointed, but general prayers will bring long lasting disappointment because believers will never know when God has heard them.

BE PERSISTENT

Another important reason why Christians struggle with belief in the effectiveness of prayer is found in Luke 11:5–8. In this passage, Christ proposed a hypothetical situation to His disciples. He said,

> "Suppose one of you shall have a friend, and shall go to him at midnight, and say to him, 'Friend, lend me three loaves; for a friend of mine has come to me from a journey, and I have nothing to set before him'; and from inside he shall answer and say, 'Do not bother me; the door has already been shut and my children and I are in bed; I cannot get up and give you anything.' I tell you, even though he will not get up and give him anything because he is his friend, yet because of his persistence he will get up and give him as much as he needs."

Christ was not saying that God the Father is a reluctant, uncaring God who has to be cajoled into action. Nor was Christ teaching that "meaningless repetition" or "many words" will get God's attention (Matt. 6:7). He was saying that "persistence" in prayer is sometimes necessary. Persistence in prayer is not for the purpose of informing God sufficiently or persuading Him to do what He does not want to do; rather, persistence in prayer is primarily for the believer's benefit.

George Müller, the great prayer warrior of the nineteenth century, explained in his autobiography that God wanted believers to persevere in prayer because "He delights in the prayers of His children." But more importantly, persistence in prayer is "to try our faith" and "to make the answer so much sweeter" when it finally comes.[3]

Many Christians do not persevere in prayer these days and therefore do not receive from God the answers they desire, which sometimes leads to disenchantment with God. There are certain things that God desires to give His followers; but He wants them to be convinced of their importance, and He wants them to really appreciate them when they arrive.

Two men in our church faithfully prayed for their aunt for about thirty years. They prayed that she would put her trust in Christ and be saved. Just recently this woman finally saw the truth of the gospel and was born again. What a thrill for these men that was, and what an encouragement to their faith and the whole church. God delayed His answer to their prayer for many years, at least from a human perspective, and as a result the faith of these men and the entire church was strengthened.

BE FREQUENT

Because Christians pray infrequently, they don't learn how to pray well. In 1 Thessalonians 5:17, Paul commanded believers to "pray without ceasing." At first glance this command seems unreasonable, even impossible. However, the verb here indicates repeated, frequent intervals of prayer, rather than constant or continuous prayer. Paul was not telling believers to pray longer but more frequently.

Many Christians have devotions once a day, which is when they pray. Many of these same Christians feel they should be praying longer during these times and feel guilty that they don't. Preachers have exhorted them to spend more time in prayer or reminded them of great saints who supposedly spent hours on their knees in prayer.

While it is important to have a time set aside for prayer each day, and that time for many could be lengthened, it is unrealistic, and not necessarily biblical, to say that Christians should be praying longer at a time. Rather than expand these times, it is more productive to pray frequently for short periods throughout the day.

John Erskine, the famous author, was fourteen when his piano teacher asked him how much time he spent practicing each day. When he told her an hour or more, he was surprised when she told him not to do that. She explained that it was unrealistic to think that he would continue to have that much time to practice as he grew older. His teacher told him to practice his piano for five to ten minutes at a time throughout the day. She said, "Spread it throughout the day, and music will become part of your life." Later Erskine followed this advice when writing his most famous work, *The Private Life of Helen of Troy*. He largely wrote it while traveling on streetcars between work and home.[4]

When Christians pray more frequent rather than longer prayers, overall they should end up talking to God more and bringing more requests to Him. As they do this, they should be giving God more opportunities to answer their prayers affirmatively. And as they see

God answering prayer, their confidence will grow and they will pray even more frequently.

Some cynic may be saying, "All that sounds great, but can it really work, practically speaking?"

In Philippians 1:3–4, Paul said to his friends in the church at Philippi, "I thank my God in all my remembrance of you, always offering prayer with joy in my every prayer for you all." In these words the apostle Paul implied how he prayed and how 1 Thessalonians 5:17 can be accomplished. When the Spirit of God brought the Philippian believers to his mind or he simply remembered them, Paul would offer up a prayer of thanks to God.

As people or situations come to the minds of Christians or the Holy Spirit reminds them, they should stop right then and briefly pray about the matter. They may not be able to pray aloud or with their eyes closed, but they can silently and quickly bring the person or situation to God. Most of the prayers in the Bible are very short, including the Lord's Prayer. This isn't just divine editing; it's God's indication of how to pray. When someone asks for prayer, believers should stop and pray immediately if at all possible. Certainly the Spirit can remind someone later, but will that person still be open and sensitive to Him? It is best to pray while things are fresh.

If Christians try to pray more by praying longer, they may become bored and dissatisfied, but if they pray more frequently, as God's Word indicates, they will be encouraged and more confident about prayer.

BE NATURAL

If Christians struggle with the length of prayers, they also strain over the language of prayer. Most Christians do not pray frankly and naturally. D. L. Moody said it best when he stated, "When I pray I am talking to God."[5] Flowery language and stained-glass window terminology will never express to God feelings and thoughts as well as simple talk.

My argument for simple words does not imply disrespect for God or deny the importance of worship in prayer. The best way to learn how to pray is to observe how people in Scripture talked with God. In the book of Habakkuk, the prophet Habakkuk spoke with God in a surprisingly frank, open, and natural fashion (Hab. 1:2–4). He was very disturbed about situations that he felt were wrong and very evil, and he didn't see God doing anything about it. The prophet asked God some very hard questions, which are in fact accusations. God did not rebuke Habakkuk for his questions, but God did not accept them as correct either. Rather he went on to answer Habakkuk's questions. Henri Nouwen has said that

> too many Christians think that prayer means to have spiritual thoughts. That's not it. Prayer means to bring into the presence of God all that you are. You can say, "God, I hate this guy; I can't stand him."
>
> The prayer of most people is too selective. They usually present only those things to God they want Him to know or think He can handle. But God can handle everything.[6]

Christians need to just talk with their heavenly Father more. They might as well tell Him what they're thinking or feeling, because He knows already. They can't hide anything. They would enjoy praying and their relationship with God more if they would be open and honest, praying simple, heartfelt prayers rather than lengthy, sanitized ones.

Howard Hendricks in his book *Taking A Stand* told about a new Christian at his very first prayer meeting. He was very reluctant to pray because he couldn't pray like the older Christians. But finally with some encouragement he prayed, "Lord, this is Jim. I'm the one that met you last Thursday night. Forgive me, Lord, because I can't say it the way the rest of these people do, but I want to tell you the best I know how. I love you, Lord. Amen." As Hendricks recalled, "He ignited the prayer meeting. We had been doing a good job of scraping the Milky Way. But he prayed."[7]

When believers don't pray naturally, simply talking with God, prayer becomes dull and unsatisfying. When they fail to pray specifically, frequently, and with persistence, they may doubt the effectiveness of prayer. Poor praying can destroy a relationship with God; and those who don't talk with God rarely talk with others about God.

CHAPTER 13

SHARING THE GOSPEL

In one church a Christian woman had married a doctor who was very antagonistic to the church and to the Christian faith. The doctor loved his wife enough to bring her to church on Sundays and to pick her up. But he never came in. The pastor made a point of being outside to greet him, but the doctor was always hostile.

Then two things happened. First, the doctor's home was badly damaged by fire. The pastor went and talked with the man and his family and offered the church's assistance. Several women from the church came over to help them clean up and wash walls. Next, the doctor's son developed an acute case of asthma and bronchitis. The boy became so sick that the doctor feared he would have to leave his practice and relocate in another area. In his despair, the doctor consented to a luncheon appointment with the pastor.

"I think he figured I'd land all over him for not coming to church," the pastor recalled. "It took a while for him to relax at that lunch. But I just told him that the people in the church were very concerned for his boy and family.

And I promised to pray for his situation. I didn't preach at him."

From that point on, the doctor softened. He asked the pastor to join him for golf. They played and talked, and a friendship grew as the pastor expressed a desire to know about the doctor's work. The doctor then began to show an interest in the church and finally attended a service with his wife. One night at home, within a month after his first visit to the church, he made a profession of faith in Christ.[1]

This is a true story that reveals an uncommon occurrence—someone concerned about another's soul. Evangelical Christians and pastors are not as involved in personal evangelism as they would like to think.

"Millions of surveys which we have helped to take around the world indicate that approximately 98 percent of the Christians do not regularly introduce others to the Savior."[2] Those were the words of Bill Bright, president of Campus Crusade for Christ. He found that only about two percent of born-again Christians were sharing the gospel regularly with unbelievers. That may be shocking to some, although it should not come as a surprise to many Christians.

A 1980 Gallup poll indicated that out of all evangelical, American believers, "only two percent had introduced another person to Christ."[3] I doubt if the statistics would be much better more than a decade later. Some may wish to argue with the accuracy of these surveys and polls, and even if the percentages are somewhat higher, most Christians are still not regularly sharing the gospel with the unsaved. Why not?

Many Christians have become discouraged about witnessing because they've seen no results from sharing their faith or they are still uncomfortable with doing it after many times. Consequently, many believers have either given up on sharing the gospel or do so only occasionally.

WATERING BEFORE REAPING

Why aren't there more positive results from witnessing? Maybe it's the "reaping mentality." Modern evangelicals have been taught and conditioned to expect quick results. They expect that when they share the gospel with an unsaved person they will reap an immediate harvest! Billy Graham shares the gospel on television and many respond. Speakers tell how they just shared the gospel with someone they had never seen before on a plane, and the person trusted Christ.

If people fail to become Christians, believers write them off as hopelessly lost, or figure someone else will have to win them to Christ, and then they still walk away wondering what went wrong. However, the Bible indicates that there usually has to be a good deal of cultivation done before someone is going to trust Christ as Savior.

In 1 Corinthians 3:6, Paul explained to the Corinthian believers that "I planted, Apollos watered, but God was causing the growth." In this verse, Paul used the metaphor of farming as an example of how the process of evangelism works. Someone has to plant the initial seed of the gospel. Then someone, or perhaps, many have to water that seed many times before there is a harvest.

One of the missionaries whom our church supports is working with Muslims. This man and his family have been extremely successful in leading Muslims to Christ. It is not an easy task. It is slow, laborious work. Yet they have seen many leave Islam and put their trust in Christ. I heard this man say that he believes a Muslim has to hear the gospel at least a hundred times before he will become a Christian.

141

Now I'm not interested in quibbling over specific numbers. The point is that unsaved people, not just Muslims, apparently have to hear the gospel repeatedly before they will trust Christ. This truth does not contradict or eliminate the sovereignty of God in the process of salvation. Obviously the nonelect will never be willing to put their trust in Christ and the elect will certainly do so (John 10:26–27).

The principle of cultivation is taught in Scripture, and it simply indicates that, in God's sovereign plan, a certain amount of "watering" will be required before any unsaved person will become a believer. The number of times that a person needs to be "watered" with the gospel message may vary. Nevertheless, the cultivation process is often longer than expected, so those who share the gospel need to think *watering* more than *reaping*. But those who witness will reap if they "do not grow weary" (Gal. 6:9). The cultivation principle just means more persistence and patience in leading others to Christ.

How does one cultivate unbelievers to Christ? It seems only reasonable and right to follow the example of the Master. How did Christ cultivate unbelievers and draw them to Himself?

Christ met unbelievers where they were. He realized what many Christians today still don't seem to understand. Cultivators have to get out in the field. "According to one count, the gospels record 132 contacts that Jesus had with people. Six were in the Temple, four in the synagogues and 122 were out with the people in the mainstream of life."[4] Regardless of the exact number, Christ was willing to meet sinners where they felt comfortable, not where He particularly wanted to be (Luke 5:27–32). It is legitimate to invite unsaved friends and relatives to church or an evangelistic crusade for purposes of harvesting what has been faithfully sown and watered, but to get unbelievers ready for harvesting, somebody must plant and water.

Even with planting and watering, some unbelievers may still not come to church. Many today see it as a money-grubbing, uncaring, and irrelevant place. They do not want any part of it. To reach these people, someone must go where they hang out.

This does not mean that Christians should try to evangelize just anywhere, and it certainly does not mean that we should participate in sin under the pretense of witnessing. Some Christians may not be mature enough to withstand temptation in certain places, and as Joe Aldrich said, "If you're made of dynamite, don't stoke blast furnaces."[5] Some Christians have weaknesses for certain sins and may always have these, so they should know their limits. Nevertheless, gospel farmers can't cultivate or reap while rocking in their favorite porch chairs.

Unbelievers will most often be reached through friendships and personal relationships. This definitely follows the example of our Lord who was called "a friend of tax-gatherers and sinners" (Luke 7:34). If witnesses approach unbelievers outside the church, they can hear the gospel presented and explained a number of times on a number of different occasions. This provides sufficient time to break down the misunderstandings unbelievers often have about Christians and Christianity and allows the Word of God and the Holy Spirit to do their convicting works.

Tim Timmons, in the book *Preaching to Convince*, told this story:

> At a tennis club one day nearly two years ago, my scheduled opponent didn't show up. Another match was arranged for me. We introduced ourselves and moved to our respective back lines to warm up.

Suddenly, the man said, "What was your name again?"

"Tim Timmons."

He dropped his racquet and moved toward the net. I met him there. With a finger pointing into my face, he asked repeatedly, "Do you know who I am?"

"No," I said, "I don't."

"Are you sure?"

"Yes, I'm sure!"

Finally he blurted out, "I'm going to tell you: I'm the porno king of Orange County! What do you think of that?"

I could tell he was waiting for me to pull a big, black Bible out of my sports bag and tear into him. I put my finger up into his face and said, "Let me ask you something. Can you play tennis?"

He gulped and eventually mumbled, "Yes!"

"Then get back there, and let's play!" I said.

We went at it. I prayed in that instance for victory (a Grade A miracle) and surprisingly, my prayers were answered.

When he shook my hand at the net, his first words were, "What times are your services Sunday?" He began attending, and in six months he retired from the pornography business. About eight months later he placed his faith in Jesus.[6]

Unbelievers need to see that Christians are not Bible thumping, boring, irrelevant people who cannot enjoy life to the fullest. As Arnold Toynbee once said, "Most people have not rejected Christianity, but a caricature."[7] This is particularly true today. Most non-Christians have a very distorted view of Christianity, thanks in part to the media coverage of born-again Christianity and the fact that there are indeed hypocrites within the ranks. Believers have to develop relationships with the unsaved; this gives the unsaved an opportunity to see that not all Christians are hypocrites. It also gives them a chance to see Christ's love.

Sometimes the love of Christ can be sufficiently communicated in one or two contacts. But, in many cases, Christ's love for the sinner has to be demonstrated over a period of time, sometimes years, before he or she is willing to accept it as unique and genuine.

Paul said in 1 Corinthians 13:1, "If I speak with the tongues of men and of angels, but do not have love, I have become a noisy gong or a clanging cymbal." This passage does not relate directly to personal evangelism; it has to do with the relationship of love to spiritual gifts. Nevertheless, the biblical principle here applies to evangelism. Evangelizing without love is as worthless as exercising speaking gifts without love (even when one has the "gift" of evangelism). The unsaved may hear words, but they won't find truth.

Now someone may say, what about the Spirit? Is He not convicting people of sin, righteousness, and judgment? (John 16:8). True, but what makes people willing to listen to what the Spirit has to say? Yes, people can be saved without a human display of love, but many will not listen to the story of Christ's love without seeing it displayed. As Joe Aldrich put it, "When love is felt, the message is heard."[8]

Donald Bubna, in his book *Building People*, told how love changed the life of Janet Landis. This dear lady grew up in a gospel-preaching church and even went to Bible college but rejected Christianity anyway. Through the efforts of what had been her home church, she eventually trusted Christ, and the love expressed for her by this congregation was, humanly-speaking, the key to it all.

Shortly before she became a Christian, she said to the pastor, "I can't explain why I'm drawn to this fellowship when I want to believe that I'm through with Christianity. . . . I'm beginning to believe that you people really care about me."[9]

God causes the growth (1 Cor. 3:6), but He has sovereignly chosen to work through people who develop relationships with the unsaved, share the gospel often, and show Christ's love to people.

When those who share the gospel think more about cultivating than reaping, they will begin to see more positive results. It might take a while, but results should come. Joe Aldrich recalled that

> a woman in Colorado read *Lifestyle Evangelism* and called to tell me that she and her husband decided to start cultivating and see what happened. They weren't, she assured me, reapers. This dear couple singled out some "worthy folks" in the husband's business network. . . . One woman seemed particularly responsive. This couple went to work and several months later I got a letter full of superlatives, punctuated with exclamation points, overflowing with joy. This non-reaping couple had just won their first convert.
>
> Their seeking friend had told them of the hurt and pain in her life. The couple listened and loved. Then one Sunday afternoon this hurting woman called and said she had to talk. The Christian lady found herself grabbing her Bible, going to the woman, and leading the lost soul to her Savior. This "reaper" was ecstatic. "I never dreamed," she said, "that I'd ever reap."[10]

When we adopt a cultivation strategy, eventually some results will come. In the meantime, how are we going to deal with the fear and discomfort we feel in witnessing?

PROPER PREPARATION

One answer to fear and discomfort is proper preparation. Many Christians are not properly prepared for sharing the Gospel, so it is something they fear to get into and something they feel uncomfortable with when they do get into it.

The first specific area of preparation has to do with mastering at least one way of presenting the gospel. It is true that there are many legitimate strategies for presenting the gospel available today and that Christ used different strategies in presenting the gospel to people in His day. Nevertheless, it is important to "distinguish between our Lord's example as an evangelist and His example as a trainer of evangelists."[11]

Christ started His disciples off with one basic strategy for evangelism (Luke 10:2–24; Matt. 10:5–23). By His example Christ demonstrated the importance of mastering at least one strategy of evangelism. As Christians grow and mature, it is fine to use other strategies as they desire and the Spirit leads. However, if Christians do not have at least one strategy mastered, it can be very discouraging to try to present the Gospel to the unsaved. This is where new believers and those who are fearful or uncomfortable should start.[12]

In addition to a good offense, believers need a good defense—an ability to defend the faith. First Peter 3:15 says that Christians should always be "ready to make a defense to everyone who asks [them] to give an account for the hope that is in [them], yet with gentleness and reverence." Christianity is a unique and reasonable faith. It does take faith to believe in Christ but not blind or irrational faith.

The empty tomb has never been adequately explained, either medically, historically, or logically, apart from the Resurrection. When people challenge

Christianity, believers should ask them to explain the empty tomb. There are several objections and questions that are commonly asked again and again by non-Christians. Paul Little found that there were essentially seven of them.[13] Christians with proper training should be able to adequately answer any of these most commonly asked questions or objections. In fact, it is their responsibility to be ready to do so.

Good offenses and defenses may convince someone that a team is worth joining, but prospective players should meet the coach. Many Christians get to the end of a gospel presentation and fail to explain how one should respond to the gospel. In other cases, the explanation of what one needs to do is extremely complicated or confusing. In either scenario, the person hearing the gospel may be unable to respond appropriately, even if he or she really wants to become a Christian.

Sometimes I hear someone present the gospel and then give an invitation to become a Christian, but I'm not sure what the presenter is suggesting and I have been a Christian for over twenty-five years. No wonder many non-Christians fail to respond to the gospel! Those hearing the gospel don't really understand what they are supposed to do! This is why it is best to simply urge unbelievers to "trust Christ." To trust Him as the One who died in their place and as the only way to heaven. Most non-Christians can understand this and can respond to this invitation either positively or negatively without confusion.

The whole issue of invitations is being hotly debated by evangelicals today. Whatever the invitation one gives to an unbeliever, it should be thoroughly biblical and completely clear.

The invitations to salvation in the New Testament predominantly use the word *belief* or *believe*,[14] such as Christ's invitation in John 5:24: "Truly, truly, I say to you, he who hears My word and believes Him who sent Me, has eternal life." However, "trust" is the essential meaning of the word *believe* when either God or Christ is the object of belief.[15] Most people understand that *trust* means dependence or reliance upon a person or object. In "trusting Christ" after the gospel has been presented, unbelievers will normally understand that they are being asked to depend upon Christ for forgiveness of sins and a way to heaven.

But what about repentance? If people understand that they are sinners worthy of eternal condemnation, and that only Christ can save them, they have in fact biblically repented.[16] Therefore, if an unbeliever decides to trust Christ alone as Savior, repentance has already occurred.

It it is best to ask people to "trust Christ" because the invitation is more likely to be effective and used by God. Those who are called are going to be eternally saved and conformed to the image of Christ (Rom. 8:29–30). None of the elect are going to be lost because of a confusing or misleading invitation to salvation, but God uses believers to draw unbelievers to Himself. What a shame if they forfeit a wonderful opportunity to reap a soul because they were too complicated, confusing, or misleading in their invitation.

If unbelievers consistently fail to respond to witnessing, this could leave some believers feeling defeated, let down by God. That is why proper preparation is so important.

RIGHT REALIZATION

In addition to proper preparation, there is a second answer to the problem of fear and discomfort in witnessing—realizing these emotions are natural and that they will never go away completely.

Some Christians think that the reason they are fearful and uncomfortable with evangelism is because they don't have the "gift." They figure that if God wanted them to regularly share the gospel He would have given them the "gift," and then they would not be afraid.

This kind of thinking is wrong because people who definitely have the gift of evangelism still feel afraid. Leighton Ford, in a *Moody Monthly* article some years ago wrote, "I'm an evangelist, and I have been witnessing and sharing my faith since I was fourteen years old. I have preached to crowds of 60,000 people, and yet I still get nervous when talking to an individual about Christ."[17]

Dawson Trotman also testified that

> I have been a Christian for twenty-nine years and it still frightens me to talk to a man about his need of salvation. Having that fear after so many years of doing personal work used to bother me. Suddenly I realized that such fear was only a little red light going on and off to remind me that it was "not by might, nor by power, but by my Spirit, saith the Lord." You never get to the place where you can do it on your own. You need Him.[18]

Christians will never get to the point where they feel totally fearless or completely comfortable talking with people about Christ, even if they have the gift. Part of the reason for this is natural; everyone fears personal rejection. However, another reason is that God wants sharers of the gospel to depend upon Him; and as they do it more, they will enjoy it more.

In 2 Timothy 4:5, Paul commanded Timothy to "do the work of an evangelist." Paul used the word *work*. Sharing the gospel is hard work, but it can be comfortable work if done often enough. When it comes to witnessing, it's important to take the advice of the TV commercial: "Just do it!"

The more believers share the Gospel, the more natural it becomes. Unless they "work" at it, it can remain very scary and uncomfortable. Lest someone think that Timothy was supposed to do this "work" because he was a pastor, the New Testament is very clear that this is the responsibility of all believers (2 Cor. 5:20).

In Acts 1:8 Christ told His disciples, "you shall receive power when the Holy Spirit has come upon you; and you shall be My witnesses both in Jerusalem, and in all Judea and Samaria, and even to the remotest part of the earth." Some may say that this commission was just for the Twelve, but if so, they did not complete it—to the remotest part of the earth. This commission to the first disciples was to be carried out to completion by later disciples, like you and me.[19]

I have always admired those organizations and leaders who require new Christians to start witnessing immediately after conversion. This is the best plan to help Christians start getting comfortable with personal evangelism.

Hudson Taylor told of a Chinese pastor who always instructed new converts to witness as soon as possible. Meeting a new convert he inquired, "Brother, how long have you been saved?"

The man answered that he had been saved for about three months.

"And how many have you won to the Savior?"

"Oh, I'm only a learner," he responded.

Shaking his head in disapproval, the pastor said, "Young man, the Lord does not expect you to be a full fledged preacher, but He does expect you to be a faithful witness. Tell me, when does a candle begin to shine—when it is half burned up?"

"No, as soon as it is lit," came the reply.

"That's right, so let your light shine right away."[20]

When believers witness to non-Christians and do not see quick results, they may despair. To avoid this Christians need to focus, not so much on reaping, but on cultivation. If they do this, results will eventually come.

Some Christians are discouraged about sharing their faith because witnessing is so stressful or uncomfortable for them. These believers need to get properly prepared to share the Gospel, and then just go out and do it! The more they share the Good News, the less fearful and more comfortable they will be, whether they have the "gift" or not.

Besides reading God's Word, praying, and witnessing, we should be fellowshipping with other Christians.

CHAPTER 14

FELLOWSHIPPING WITH EACH OTHER

Not long ago, a young Russian who was a believer received a temporary visa to visit relatives in Canada. At the end of her stay, her relatives and friends expected her to defect and seek asylum in Canada or the United States. Instead she was anxious to get home. She told all who would listen that Christians in the West were too busy with material things and not interested enough in people. She said that in Russia believers really needed and wanted to be with each other.[1]

Christians in the West can either write this young lady off as just being nationalistic, or they can take a long, hard look at themselves and their churches and see that she has a point. I have made two trips to the former Soviet Union and can testify to the truth of what she said. Many believers today are not involved with each other in true biblical fellowship. Oh, they have friends who are fellow Christians and they attend "fellowships" after church on Sunday nights, but many born-again Christians are not often involved in true biblical fellowship on the human level.

The word *fellowship* in Scripture means "close, personal relationships or associations,"[2] not casual acquaintances or shallow friendships.

> The true nature of Christian fellowship may be clarified by contrasting the use of two German words. The first, *Gesellschaft*, refers to people thrown together without deep ties, such as all the people riding the same bus. The second, *Gemeinschaft*, refers to those with intimate ties of family or community.[3]

True, biblical fellowship is not *just* friendship, but *close* friendships like that experienced by members of the same family.

Non-Christians can have extremely close friendships, but biblical fellowship has a spiritual dimension that makes it radically different from the intimate associations of the unsaved.

FELLOWSHIP WITH GOD

First John 1:3 teaches that there are two levels of biblical fellowship. The first, and most important, is fellowship with God. This verse indicates that all Christians have fellowship with God. As John said, "indeed our fellowship is with the Father, and His Son Jesus Christ." If a person has been born-again, he has "fellowship," i.e., a personal relationship with God. However, the *quality* and *closeness* of that relationship is dependent upon such things as the believer confessing his sins (1 John 1:9). The closeness of a person's relationship to God also depends on his relationship to other believers, which is the second level of biblical fellowship.

In 1 John 1:3, John indicated his desire for his Christian readers to have "fellowship" with him. True spiritual fellowship begins with a personal relationship to God, but then that opens up the possibility for close relationships with other Christians.

FELLOWSHIP WITH OTHERS

It is the spiritual aspect of Christian fellowship that bonds believers together and makes biblical fellowship unique. Because Christians are connected with the true God, they can form friendships quickly and deeply. The world's relationships can be close, but not as close. The friendships among non-Christians are limited in ways that Christian fellowship is not.

At a college summer retreat out in the mountains of California soon after World War II, among those present were a young man who had flown in Hitler's Luftwaffe, another who had flown with the Japanese, and a third who had been in the US Air Force and had bombed the cities of Germany. None of these knew that the others were present at the retreat, nor did they know each other, and none was a Christian. At the final meeting, any person who chose to accept Christ and give his life to serve the Savior tossed a stick of wood on a bonfire, symbolizing that his life would now be given to burn for Christ. First, the German stood to accept Christ, walked to the fire and threw a stick in; a few moments later, the Japanese; then following him, the American pilot, all receiving the Lord Jesus Christ. Then the three exwar pilots, with their arms around each other and tears streaming down their faces, sang with all those present, "Blessed be the tie that binds our hearts in Christian love."[4]

Cults are attracting large numbers of people today who have grown up in churches, even some evangelical

Christian churches. What a lot of these people are looking for are deep ties and friendships like those found in a family. They apparently have not found these in their churches. No wonder the cults emphasize this. For instance, a large sign just inside the entrance of a Unification Church center in a major city proclaims: "Welcome Home!"[5]

Christians need to acknowledge this problem and do something about it. People are desperately looking for true fellowship, and some are willing to go wherever they have to in order to find it. Of course, outside of the true Christian community, they will only receive a pale imitation of the real thing.

The first reason why believers are not always involved in biblical fellowship on a human level is because they don't understand that "fellowship" is more than simple friendship. It is a close, personal relationship with others who share the same faith.

The second reason why Christians are not always involved in biblical fellowship on a human level is because they are not quite sure how to make it happen. They are uncertain about how to develop close, personal relationships with fellow Christians.

The Scripture never once commands believers to "fellowship" with one another, but the New Testament *rarely* commands believers to witness or share their faith. (Acts 1:8 would be one example I can find.) Yet most Christians don't doubt their responsibility to do that. The New Testament clearly indicates that fellowship on the human level is definitely something that should be happening (1 John 1:3; Acts 2:42). So how does it happen? The Bible gives us both general and specific examples.

When early Christians fellowshipped, they mutually shared or participated with one another in an event or certain actions.[6] The early church fellowshipped by partaking of the Lord's Supper together,[7] through corporate prayer, by sharing their physical possessions and property, and through eating together in their homes (Acts 2:42–46).

Fellowship was something that the early church continually devoted themselves to, along with the apostles' teaching, breaking bread, and prayer (Acts 2:42). All were equally important to the spiritual health and growth of the church. However, biblical fellowship does not just happen through general sharing between believers. It does not necessarily happen as a result of participating in meals with fellow Christians. More specifically, true fellowship happens when Christians mutually share what Christ is doing in their lives.

In 2 Corinthians 1:8–10, Paul gave a beautiful example of fellowship. He shared with the Corinthian believers how God "delivered" him "from so great a peril of death" and how the Corinthians helped him through their prayers. While Paul's relationship with the Corinthians was somewhat strained for a number of reasons, as is clear from the remainder of the book, here he was seeking to build a closer relationship with these believers by sharing what God had done for him through them. This is authentic fellowship.

In order for Christians to have true fellowship and share what God is doing in their lives, they first have to think about what He's actually doing. Unless they take the time to recognize what God is doing with them and through them, they will not be able to fellowship.

Not only that, but they have to work at reaching out to other Christians and being vulnerable. When they get together for worship at church or even in small groups for Bible study and prayer, they may not experience fellowship unless they seek out other believers.

Many churches do not plan opportunities for fellow-ship. If they do, often they do not know how to facilitate it. Believers can bemoan this weakness of the contemporary church, but they should not allow institutional structures to stifle fellowship. It's up to every believer to make it happen.

Opening up to others can be scary, but fellowship is not about sharing personal matters. As Crabb and Allender have put it:

> Christian fellowship is not designed to be a forum for revealing personal problems; rather, it is an opportunity to share with others the relevance of Christ's life to ours. This does require self-disclosure and openness, not as an end itself, but as a means to the end of knowing Christ more fully.[8]

If believers share themselves, they can get hurt. Developing close relationships always involves risk. Andy Warhol once said, "I stopped caring so much about having close relationships . . . You can only be hurt if you care a lot."[9] However, the risk is worth it. Many people deeply hurt the apostle Paul (2 Tim 4:14), and yet he did not let that keep him from fellowshipping and developing close relationships.

In 1 Corinthians 16:17–18, Paul said, "And I rejoice over the coming of Stephanas and Fortunatus and Achaicus; because they have supplied what was lacking on your part. For they have refreshed my spirit. . . ." The word *refresh* means "give [someone] rest."[10] Society today may leave believers tired physically, emotionally, and spiritually, but when they fellowship—really fellowship—with other believers, they will come away from the experience relaxed and encouraged. If Christians leave a gathering drained and empty, it is possible that they have been simply socializing rather than fellowshipping.

Real fellowship draws Christians closer to each other and to God. When believers fail to fellowship with others, the Christian life can become difficult, seemingly impossible. To avoid disappointment believers have to be involved in spiritual exercise, including developing a working knowledge of God's Word, prayer, sharing the gospel, and true fellowship. Some don't because they are false professors; others because they are wayward believers. The church must love both groups—recognizing the unsaved and restoring the saved.

PART 5

WHEN CHRISTIANS SIN

CHAPTER 15

RECOGNIZING FALSE PROFESSORS, FALSE TEACHERS, AND APOSTATES

Not too long ago I was encouraged by a lady from my church to share the gospel with a young man who was dating her daughter. She felt that he would be open to a gospel presentation, and when I called him, indeed he was. I met with this young man for a couple of hours, getting to know him personally, and then carefully explaining the Good News about Jesus Christ to him. At the end of the gospel presentation I asked him if he was willing to trust Christ as his Savior. He immediately said yes. We prayed together and I sincerely believed that he had entered into God's family. However, when I sent one of the elders from our church to follow up on him, this new "Christian" kept putting him off. Later on when I talked with him personally, he professed to be a Christian, but he could not explain to me in any intelligible fashion what it meant to be a

Christian. Since that time it has come to light that his "conversion" did not result in any spiritual fruit that could be observed, and I have had to conclude that this man is almost certainly "a professor, but not a possessor."

John Piper in his book *Desiring God* stated,

> We are surrounded by unconverted people who think they do believe in Jesus. Drunks on the street say they believe. Unmarried couples sleeping together say they believe. Elderly people who haven't sought worship or fellowship for forty years say they believe. All kinds of lukewarm, world-loving church attenders say they believe. The world abounds with millions of unconverted people who say that they believe in Jesus.[1]

There are undoubtedly many people in the world today, and especially in the United States, who call themselves "Christians," but who are not truly born again. This should not surprise us, because this was also true in Christ's day.

One day, Christ was speaking in the synagogue in Capernaum, and He told all who were listening that "he who eats My flesh and drinks My blood has eternal life" (John 6:54). This caused quite a stir among those listening, including Christ's "disciples" (v. 60–61). The final result was that "many of His disciples withdrew, and were not walking with Him anymore" (v. 66).

Here were people who professed to "believe" in Jesus and were following Him as "disciples," but who then left Christ, never to return. What was the problem? Were they unwilling to accept the lordship of Christ? Not according to the passage. Were the rigors of discipleship too much for them to endure? Apparently not. The problem was that they had never truly believed that Christ was the Savior and the Messiah. In fact, Christ told them that "there are some of you who do not believe" (v. 64).

For some time these people followed Christ and claimed to be His disciples, but when they finally understood the essence of Christ's message, they rejected it and Him. When they said, "This is a difficult statement; who can listen to it" (v. 60), they really meant, "Who can accept it?" They were unwilling to accept Christ as their Savior and Messiah. There are always people around who claim to be Christians, but who actually are not.

First of all, there are false teachers as well as false professors. False teachers are different from false professors because they deliberately misrepresent themselves as true believers for various reasons. Sometimes false teachers pretend to be believers in order to gain sex, money, or fame. Jude warned about this in his letter (Jude 16). But in many cases false teachers claim to be Christians so that they can spread false doctrine.

Recently, some Mormon missionaries showed up at our Wednesday night service, claiming to simply be "Christians" who were looking for a place for worship and fellowship with other believers. Their real motive, however, became apparent when they began to contact people from our church. They were seeking people to convert to Mormonism. I arranged a meeting with them and told them they were not to enter our services again or contact our people. They left my office still insisting that they were "Christians" who meant no harm. They were false teachers, not just false professors.

When we know someone is not a Christian but is pretending to be one for sinful reasons, then Paul says we are to "turn away from them" (Romans 16:17–18).

However, false professors are people who think that they are saved, but who have not truly believed. They may have faith, but that faith is deficient and/or defective.

False professors sometimes have a problem understanding that they are sinners who are totally lost. They may be "trusting" in Christ, but these people are also trusting in their good works. Thus their faith in Christ is deficient. They are not trusting in Christ alone to get to heaven. Others who are false professors realize they are sinners, but they do not understand that Christ's death totally paid for all their sins. Thus their faith is defective because they believe that they have to do good works in order to make up the difference. So false professors do not completely or correctly understand the gospel message, and it is our reponsibility as Christians to help them comprehend it.

Now it is true that the Holy Spirit is ultimately the one who "convicts" people about their sinfulness as well as the righteousness found in Christ (John 16:8–11). If it were not for Him, not one person would ever come to a clear understanding of what the gospel message is all about. Nevertheless, God has sovereignly decided to use people who faithfully present the Word of God as a part of this process (Rom. 10:14). Keeping this in mind, when believers discern false professors, how should they approach them?

ASKING THE RIGHT QUESTION

First, they should not go to these people and accuse them of not being true Christians, or even directly question whether they are saved. It is entirely possible to be mistaken in this regard and to unnecessarily offend either a believer or someone who thinks they are saved. If the accusing believer is wrong, it could severely damage the assurance of a sinning Christian. It also could cost the believer the opportunity to present the gospel to an unbeliever.

Christ was very candid with the false professors in John 6 about their unbelief. However, Christ is God and knows all things. He knows the hearts and minds of people; believers do not. They must proceed much more carefully. Developing a relationship with a supposed false professor may clear up doubts about his spiritual status. If a relationship with the person in question does not clarify matters, then a discussion about spiritual things is in order, and in particular, the now classic question: "(person's name), if you were to die tonight, and stand before God, and He asked you why He should let you into heaven, what would you tell Him?"[2] This question has an amazing ability to sort out professors from possessors.

Many times in my personal ministry I have talked with people who said they were Christians and even talked about faith in Christ, but when I asked them this question I received an answer that clearly indicated that they were not trusting in Christ alone to get them into heaven. Some are really trusting in good works or Christ plus good works, and some can't even answer the question, which indicates that they haven't really thought through the issue. It's amazing how confused or deceived people can be about their standing with God, even people in good, Bible-believing, gospel-preaching churches. A gentleman in the March 1987 issue of *Moody Monthly* tells about an encounter with just such a person:

Less than a year ago, I was helping a friend counsel someone on the brink of divorce. My friend noticed a hearse go by and asked the counselee an adapted version of "the Kennedy Question". . . . "If that were your body in that hearse, do you know you would be in heaven?" I thought he was wasting time. I mean, the man with the bad marriage was raised in a Christian home, attended a fundamental church, had spent a couple of years in Bible college. Why not save evangelism for someone who needed it? The answer was sure and immediate, just as I knew it would be. "Yes, I know I would be in heaven." Good, I thought, let's get on with the marriage counseling. But my friend wasn't through. "On what basis?" Again the answer was quick and sure. "On the basis of my works." I laughed. It was a joke, right? The classic answer was so opposite of the truth that it had to be a put-on. My laughter died when I could see in his eyes that he was serious. Over the next several minutes we asked and probed, finally establishing that what he had understood from all those years of sitting under the preaching of the gospel was that he had to earn his way into heaven.[3]

Asking people on what basis they expect to get into heaven is usually non-threatening and revealing, particularly if a believer has established a friendship with the individual. Of course, it is appropriate and right for a pastor from the pulpit to regularly remind the people that it is entirely possible for some of them to be professors but not possessors, and to issue a general challenge to "test yourselves to see if you are in the faith" (2 Cor. 13:5), and to then go on to clearly explain the gospel.

MAKING THE MESSAGE PLAIN

It is not appropriate to confuse people about the gospel by giving them a gospel presentation that includes issues that are not an integral part of the offer of salvation. John MacArthur quoted a friend as saying that "the contemporary church often fails to present the Gospel clearly enough for the non-elect to reject it."[4] I have no doubt that this is true to a certain extent. But it is also true that the contemporary church has sometimes made the gospel so complex or confusing that even the elect reject it, at least in those instances.

The United States Defense Department in its service manual gives a recipe for canned fruitcake to be served to its personnel. This recipe takes up eighteen pages![5]

Leave it to the Pentagon to make something relatively simple into something incredibly complex. However, many today are doing the same thing with the gospel. The gospel message is relatively simple, but many insist on making it unnecessarily complex.

It is true that Christ sometimes discussed discipleship along with a simple offer of salvation, but this was not always the case (see John 3–4). When Christ discussed discipleship along with the gospel, He kept the issues in the correct order (salvation first, discipleship second). He also presented discipleship in gentle and encouraging terms (Matt. 11:28–30).

On the occasions when Christ challenged his disciples about their level of commitment to Him, His purpose was not to add conditions to the simple gospel message but to demonstrate that those being challenged were either unbelievers (Mark 10:17–23; Luke 9:57–62), or if they were true disciples, they were not following Him as faithfully as they should (John 21:15–19).

S. Lewis Johnson, Jr. recently put it well when he said,

> The glory of the gospel of grace and a limited response do not seem compatible, but the solution is not to be found in inducing shallow professions that do not last by the questionable methods of "decisional evangelism" or by introducing sterner demands that have problematic biblical support. Let us remember that our sovereign God alone saves souls, and He can be trusted with that work. Let us do our work of preaching His saving Word. Lewis Sperry Chafer used to exhort his students (all men in those days), "Men, preach an accurate Gospel!" That's still good counsel. Then the results may be left safely with the Lord.[6]

When believers present the gospel clearly to someone they think is a false professor, that person may still fail to grasp the full implications of the gospel. They should continue to present the truth to them tactfully and lovingly until they understand what the gospel is all about. When the truth finally sinks in, these people will either truly trust Christ, or as some did in John 6, they will leave, never to return. When people who once claimed to be Christians deny Christ and walk away, they are "apostates." This means they have departed from, or rebelled against, the truth. This brings up an important question: Can a true Christian become an apostate?

DEALING WITH DOUBTS AND DENIALS

A man named Skip Porteous recently wrote an autobiographical work entitled *Jesus Doesn't Live Here Anymore*. Years ago this man professed Christ as Savior, went to Bible college, did evangelistic work in Southern California, and pastored two churches. But since then he has totally repudiated his faith in Jesus Christ. Today he is adamant in his opposition to Christ and evangelical Christianity.[7]

Regardless of what the title of his book says, the Bible indicates that Jesus Christ was never truly involved in this man's life.

In 1 John 2:18–23, John explained that certain people left the fellowship of Christians and denied the deity of Christ. These people were apostates. They fellowshipped with true believers for a while and perhaps appeared to bear real spiritual fruit, but then suddenly left. John said, "They were not really of us" (1 John 2:19). These apostates never really believed in Christ, although they claimed to do so for a while.

The scriptural answer to the question then is no. However, that does not mean that a true Christian will always or completely be free of doubt. Doubt is a very real possibility for a Christian (James 1:6–8), but there are different kinds of doubt.

First, Christians can have doubts about whether or not they are really saved (1 John 3:19–20). Christians can also have doubts about God, whether or not He really cares or really keeps His Word. There is nothing in Scripture that indicates that those doubts will last only a few moments or even a short period of time. Christians can have doubts about themselves or God that go on for indefinite, but significant periods of time. Though Christians may have doubts, true believers will never completely or permanently lose their faith in God.[8]

Over the years I have talked with many people who tell me with great sincerity and conviction that they believe Christ died for their sins, and that they are trusting in Christ because of that to get them to heaven. They believe that God loved them and sent His Son so that they can have a home in heaven, but, in the same breath, some of these same people admit that they have severe doubts about God's love for them at that moment. They are disappointed with God and/or the Christian life. Consequently, these people are often consciously sinning. But they have not totally abandoned their faith in God or Christ.

Now there are some who believe that Christians can totally and permanently lose their faith and deny Christ as their Savior.

Christians can in moments of weakness deny Christ; Peter did it, and he was one of the greatest servants of God ever (Mark 14:66–72). But even though a true believer may momentarily or temporarily deny Christ, that person will soon set the record straight as did Peter. The reason true Christians cannot and will not totally and permanently deny Christ is because God will not let them. As 1 Thessalonians 5:24 says, "faithful is He who calls you, and He also will bring it to pass."

Sheldon Vanauken understood the faithfulness of God. While still a young man and a young Christian, his wife, "Davy," died of a terrible disease. This tragic incident caused him to have serious doubts about God. He wondered why God would allow such a tragedy to happen. As he remembers in his book, *A Severe Mercy*:

> The world was still empty without Davy, and now God seemed to have withdrawn, too. My sense of desolation increased. God could not be as loving as He was supposed to be, or—the other alternative. One sleepless night, drawing on to morning, I was overwhelmed with a sense of cosmos empty of God as well as Davy. "All right," I muttered to myself. "To hell with God. I'm not going to believe this damned rubbish anymore. Lies, all lies. I've been had." Up I sprang and rushed out to the country. This was the end of God. Ha!
>
> And then I found I *could not* reject God. I could not. I cannot explain this. One discovers one cannot move a boulder by trying with all one's strength to do it. I discovered—without any sudden influx of love or faith— that I could not reject Christianity. Why I don't know. There it was. I could not.[9]

There are some people who pretend to be Christians in order to take advantage of believers or to present false doctrine to them. They are false teachers. However, many people in the world today, even in evangelical churches today, are false professors. These people are living sinful lives because they do not really understand the gospel and thus have never truly accepted it.There are others who have left the church and denied Christ who are also living sinful lives.

These are apostates. There is still another group in the church today who profess Christ and demonstrate some spiritual life, but are also consciously sinning. These people are disappointed and disillusioned Christians. They have not completely lost their faith nor will they. But they are struggling with trusting God on a daily basis. What can and should be done to help these brothers and sisters in Christ?

CHAPTER 16

RESTORING WAYWARD CHRISTIANS

D on Rosenberger, a sailor stationed at Pearl Harbor during World War II, trusted Christ as his Savior on 8 October 1943 and subsequently became very involved with Dawson Trotman and his fledgling Navigator's ministry. Working his way up to one of Dawson's "lieutenants," he continued for many years to serve the Lord with the Navigators; he also trained counselors for Billy Graham Crusades. In 1953 he left the Navigators to become director of the Christian Youth Crusade. At this time he was also attending graduate school and pastoring a church.

Over a period of twenty years he drifted out of a close, personal relationship with God. He separated from his wife, pursued a career as a financial consultant, and became satisfied with himself and his life.[1]

The problem of conscious sinning and uncommitted living for Christ by someone like Don is not unique to contemporary Christianity and is an example of an increasing number of wayward Christians.

D. L. Moody said many years ago, "we are suffering more today from professed Christians who have either gone to sleep or who have never waked up, than from any one cause."[2]

Hannah Whitall Smith said in 1875:

> The standard of practical holy living has been so low among Christians that very often the person who tries to practice spiritual disciplines in everyday life is looked upon with disapproval by a large portion of the church. And for the most part, the followers of Jesus Christ are satisfied with a life so conformed to the world, and so like it in almost every respect, that to a casual observer there is no difference between the Christian and the pagan.[3]

The fact that a straying Christian is an old problem for the church does not make it any more acceptable. Some do profess Christ without truly possessing Him, but what about those who are disappointed with God, fellow Christians, or the Christian life in general? How can we help these wayward believers?

ENCOURAGING AND EXHORTING

First of all, it is the believer's reponsibility to help these brothers and sisters in Christ. In Galatians 6:1, Paul addressed himself to all the "brethren," not just church leaders. He went on to say that those who are "spiritual" have the responsibility to "restore" anyChristians who are caught in a trespass.

The word *caught* indicates that a person is ensnared or overpowered by a certain sin, and that without help they are unlikely to escape it. We who are "spiritual" must come to their aid. This term *spiritual* does not refer to complete spiritual maturity or "having it all together." It simply indicates in the context that if one is "walk[ing] by the Spirit" (Gal. 5:25) and sees someone ensnared in sin, the person walking by the Spirit is obligated to help.

The type of help required is indicated by the word *restore*. It has the idea of returning someone or something to its original state, and is used in the sense of mending or resetting a broken bone.[4] This word not only indicates that the process is one of restoration rather than punishment, but it also indicates that the process will be initially painful. It will hurt both parties, but it is necessary for the healing to begin.

Before we approach a Christian who is ensnared in sin, we should try if possible to develop a friendship with him, or at least communicate to him in a concrete way that we care about him; otherwise we cannot expect him to listen to us. We have to go to him, as Galatians 6:1 says, "in a spirit of gentleness," which involves "speaking the truth in love" (Eph. 4:15).

What we should say to a believer caught in sin is not indicated by Galatians 6:1. I believe that is because Paul knew that every situation is different. We cannot and should not approach everyone in exactly the same manner. If a believer is unconsciously sinning, loving exhortation is in order and should be sufficient.

We need to remind believers of Romans 12:1, where Paul exhorts them to present their bodies a "living and holy sacrifice." This is both reasonable and right in light of "the mercies of God" that have been shown to them.

A further reminder of 1 Corinthians 6:20 would probably also be helpful, where Paul says, "You have been bought with a price. Therefore glorify God in your body." We have no right as Christians to live as we see fit. We now belong to God, who has bought us with the precious blood of His Son, Jesus Christ (1 Pet. 1:18–19). There is an interesting illustration of this truth in *David Frost's Book of the World's Worst Decisions*:

In 1910 Olav Olavson, a Swedish citizen, fell upon hard times and decided to sell his body for medical research to the Karolinska Institute in Stockholm. The following year he inherited a fortune and resolved to buy himself back. The institute refused to sell its rights to his body, went to court, and won possession of it. Moreover, the institute obtained damages, since Olav had two teeth pulled out without asking their permission as ultimate owners of his body.[5]

While God has no problem with us getting a tooth pulled if necessary, a true Christian knows that Jesus is Lord and that from the standpoint of the cross, Christ deserves his allegiance, service, loyalty, and obedience. Believers who are sinning need to be reminded of this truth both personally and from evangelical pulpits. Nevertheless, exhortations to acknowledge Christ's lordship and to obey Him may not be enough to turn them back if the problem is disappointment or disillusionment.

As discussed before, Christians who are consciously sinning are disappointed or disillusioned with God, the Christian life, fellow believers, or all three. These believers have not forgotten what God did for them at the cross, but they are wondering why things are so apparently wrong or bad now. In order to restore these believers, encouragement will be necessary.

In Hebrews 3:13, the writer of Hebrews commands us to "encourage one another day after day, as long as it is still called 'today,' lest any one of you be hardened by the deceitfulness of sin."

When we encounter a fellow believer who is ensnared in sin but has little interest in escape because of disappointment or disillusionment, it is important that we encourage that person before they become hardened against God by it.

Encouraging someone takes time, and it begins with finding out why wayward believers are disillusioned with Christianity. Those who want to help must probe gently and listen intently. People away from God often do not want to admit it, or sometimes they simply cannot verbalize their problems. They know something is wrong, but they can't figure out what it is, so they blame God.

Encouragers must pinpoint problems and then lead sinning Christians back to God's Word for an understanding of what happened and what God was doing at the time a certain problem began. Although encouragers cannot perfectly know God's mind, they can make general observations based on Scripture and God's character. These new perspectives from God's Word should turn on some lights for disappointed Christians.

After caring Christians diagnose root problems, they should then lovingly exhort erring believers to trust God completely and to do what is right. The fact that discouraged believers often feel that God has betrayed them should be understood and acknowledged. Nevertheless, once the misunderstanding is cleared up, the responsibility of these struggling believers is to obey God. The restorer must not stop with encouragement. Exhortation must follow to motivate lapsed believers to do what they must do.

It would be nice if sinful and uncommitted Christians would respond immediately and positively to restoration efforts. Why don't they? One reason is that concerned restorers can be wrong about the spiritual state of sinning Christians. The possibility also exists that some Christians have never truly understood the gospel and are not saved. If they are saved, it is also possible that the real reason for their disillusionment has not yet been uncovered. Perhaps they were not initially approached "in a spirit of gentleness" and love, and therefore they are still very disillusioned and perhaps even more so than before.

Whatever the reasons Christians are leading sinful and uncommitted lives, other believers should not give up on them. They should continue to love them and if possible encourage and exhort them. Above all, they should be balanced in their approoach to wayward believers. Over-exhortation may drive them away, but encouragement without diagnosis of the real issues may resolve nothing.

DISCIPLINING

If encouragement and exhortation doesn't work, what about church discipline? Where does it fit into this process? Should every Christian be immediately and formally disciplined by the church for any conscious sin? I used to think so, but I had a hard time reconciling this with 1 Thessalonians 5:14, which says to "help the weak." The word *weak* here refers not to physical weakness but to spiritual,[6] and *help* means literally "to hold one's self over against."[7] In other words, mature believers are to support spiritually weak Christians by keeping them from getting into sin or falling further into sin. The spiritually weak are believers who desire to do what is right, but they lack the discipline to follow through. Usually they are new Christians; however, these people can also be believers who because of their sinful past continue to struggle with certain sins. Occasional encouragement and exhortation alone will not be enough to turn these believers around. They will require constant supervision and support to keep them from sinning.

This initial approach does not preclude formal church discipline or excuse sin. In 2 Thessalonians 3:6, Paul said, "Now we command you, brethren, in the name of our Lord Jesus Christ, that you keep aloof from every brother who leads an unruly life and not according to the tradition which you received from us." Christians who lead "unruly" lives are to be disciplined; however, what does "unruly" mean? It is a military term that means to be "out of step."[8]

In verses 7–13, "unruly" Christians are those out of step with the church, an unnecessary "burden." Their sin is open and obvious, disrupting the entire church. These people are to be exhorted to do what is right (1Thess. 5:14; 2 Thess. 3:12), and if they don't they are not to be associated with (v. 14).

Paul did not say to excommunicate them. That discipline is reserved for sexually immoral believers (1 Cor. 5:1), those causing divisions (Titus 3:10), and teachers of false doctrines (Rom. 16:17). Rather, other believers are not to "associate" with unruly Christians so that they "may be put to shame" (2 Thess. 3:14). The word *associate* refers to Christian fellowship or social mingling.[9] When sin affects the entire local body adversely, the welfare of the church has to come before the interests of individuals, no matter who they are or how much some may care about them. Nevertheless, Paul also said, "Do not regard" them as enemies, "but admonish" them as brothers (2 Thess. 3:15).

We have a definite responsibility to restore erring Christians. God expects us to do our part and He uses us as we do so; however, God's part in restoration is more crucial than ours. In fact, we may come to the point where we cannot do anything else, and God has to take over completely.

In John 15:1–2, the apostle John quoted Jesus as having said that "I am the true vine, and my Father is the vinedresser. Every branch in Me that does not bear fruit, He takes away." R. K. Harrison believes that this phrase translated "takes away" is best translated "lifts up."[10] As Joseph Dillow pointed out, this is the way this word is used in at least eight out of twenty-four occurrences in the Gospel of John.[11] "Lift up" is a possible meaning for this word[12] because it is a standard practice in vineyards to lift up fallen vines so that they can begin to bear fruit again.

GOD'S ROLE

When Christians are consciously sinning and not bearing fruit, God at some point steps in to lift them up. Why He does not do this immediately is hidden in His own wise and loving purposes. God has several different ways to bring the wayward believer back to the fold.

In 1 Kings 19:2–18 God restored one of His prophets. The prophet Elijah was a part of God's great victory on Mt. Carmel (1 Kings 18), and it appeared as if everything was going great. But then Jezebel vowed to take Elijah's life and he fled, discouraged and scared. He actually pleaded with God to take his life! That's how disillusioned he was.

God demonstrated His love and concern for Elijah (vv. 5–7)by sending an angel to feed him twice, and once it was "the angel of the LORD" the Son of God. God also allowed him to sleep so that he could get his strength back. He had to realize that God was graciously providing for him.

Sometimes God so visibly demonstrates His great love for fallen believers that the problem quickly goes away. Disappointed believers become convinced that God really loves and cares about them. God's provision was not sufficient for Elijah, so God overwhelmed him with a tremendous display of His power (vv. 8–14).

Elijah traveled forty days and nights to Mt. Horeb, which is also known as Mt. Sinai. It was here that Moses received the Ten Commandments and saw the glory of God (Ex. 33:17–23). In the very same cave, Elijah stood by as God dazzled him with a tremendous display of His power. First a strong wind, then an earthquake, and finally a fire.

Sometimes God impresses erring Christians with His incredible power so that whatever disappointed them is no longer a problem. Those who wondered what in the world God was doing, or if God was really in control, suddenly realize that God is able to do whatever He desires and that God is doing just that. In Elijah's case, even God's power was not enough, so God encouraged him with the support of other godly men (vv. 15–18).

Elijah was sent by God to anoint two new kings who would help him in his campaign against Baal worship. God also instructed him to anoint another prophet, Elisha, who would help and support him, and eventually succeed him. Finally, God informed Elijah that there were still seven thousand people in Israel who were loyal to the true God. All of this was carefully calculated to encourage Elijah by showing him that God really was supporting him.

Sometimes God encourages the discouraged believer with wonderful displays of His support. When this happens that person is no longer disappointed because he sees that God is helping him and will continue to do so.

As a result of God manifesting His love, power, and support, Elijah was restored and went back to faithfully serving God with his life.

Unfortunately, even when God clearly displays His love, power, and support, some wayward believers fail to come back. Then God has to take more painful measures.

In Hebrews 12:4–11, the writer of Hebrews warned that those "whom the Lord loves He disciplines" (v. 6). God disciplines those who belong to Him when they refuse to do what is right. In fact, He even "scourges" those who require more severe discipline. The word *scourge* may refer to a whip lashing. How God does this varies from person to person; He knows how to get a person's attention and lash him where it will be most effective in bringing him back.

The fact that God disciplines a person is a clear indication that he is part of God's family (v. 7). If a person continues to consciously sin and there is no severe discipline forthcoming, it indicates that that person is illegitimate (v. 8).

Normally, when God disciplines a person, "it yields the peaceful fruit of righteousness" (v. 11). However, there are some erring believers who still will not respond.

God's plans never fail. When He sets out to restore a wayward believer, He does so. But God may have to bring that person home to glory to do it. If a Christian continues to refuse a close walk with God on earth, then God brings him home to heaven where complete restoration does occur.[13]

I have often wondered why God does not seem to call Christians home more often who are consciously sinning. It doesn't appear that God is really doing this on a regular basis, but maybe He is. It may not always be apparent who is willfully sinning, and only God knows why Christians die when they do. And if He lets sinning Christians live, it is because He is incredibly gracious and longsuffering. Undoubtedly He puts up with people and their sin much longer than His followers would. Believers cannot discount the grace of God nor presume upon it.

THE BELIEVER'S PART

When God restores a wayward believer to a renewed life for Him on this earth, He expects others to get involved, to start up the discipling process. As Bill Hull said:

> All Christians have a desire to grow, please God, and make their lives count. The desire surfaces periodically; the pastor/coach looks for those teachable moments and claims them as precious jewels of opportunity. The Christian becomes inspired by a sermon, reading Scripture, or a conversation. The event causes him to renew his commitment to grow. But desire without discipline derails good intentions.[14]

If faithful Christians don't properly disciple revived believers, they can become disappointed again with God, other Christians, or the Christian life. That's why the words of Robert Coleman must ring true for every believer: "Discipling men and women is the priority around which our lives should be oriented."[15]

In November of 1980, Don Rosenberger agreed to meet with an old friend, Doug Sparks. He and Doug had served the Lord together in the Navigator ministry thirty years earlier. Don could not bring himself to turn down his friend's request for a meeting, but he was very apprehensive about it.

On the arranged weekend, Doug Sparks and Don traveled together to Cape Cod. As they drove along, Don admitted to Doug that he was not "in fellowship with the Lord." At first Don said that this was because he had changed some of his thinking about Christ and God's Word. But then he went on to confess that he had suffered with some "profound disillusionments and disappointments."

As Don talked, Doug continued to simply listen. It came out that Don had been deeply hurt, particularly by Dawson Trotman of Navigators. Dawson was a tremendous servant of God, but like all of us, had weaknesses. As Don continued sharing, he began to sob. Doug kept on listening through the tears, but finally he put his finger on what needed to be done in order for Don to be whole again. He asked Don if he had ever really forgiven Dawson Trotman in his heart for what had happened. Don did not respond, but he began to ponder Doug's words and his question.

The morning after his long talk with Doug Sparks, Don rose early to go down to the beach. He wanted to avoid Doug if possible, but he could not avoid God. As Don walked along the ocean, he began to talk with God—really talk with God. As he did, he began to cry uncontrollably. Later on he told Doug at breakfast, "It was as though scales dropped from my eyes and I could see again the way I did twenty years ago."

When Don got back home, he called his wife, Eleanor, and told her what incredible things God had done in his life. A few days later they had a tearful reunion and began the process of restoring their marriage.

Don Rosenberger is now living faithfully for the Lord, and God continues to work in his life in a marvelous fashion. In the same way, He will work in ours if we humbly admit our need of Him.

CONCLUSION

A young father trusted Christ and began to attend church regularly. For a number of years he lived a normal life, loved his wife and kids, and generally conducted himself in an exemplary way, yet something was missing in his life. He wasn't routinely sinning, but he wasn't actively living for the Lord either. Satisfaction in the Christian life eluded him, and for a number of years he didn't make progress.

Four or five years ago the example of his wife and family encouraged him to devote himself more fully to God. This kindled a spiritual spark, and he joined a men's discipleship group for a year. He participated in a men's leadership group the next year and began serving God in earnest. Now this man is an elder in our church and a fine servant of God who truly enjoys his close relationship with the Lord. Those who have seen his development over the last several years are delighted by what God has done through biblical discipleship.

New Christians need discipleship and so do fallen believers, but indifferent followers of God need it, too. Some Christians are disappointed with God, but many are simply ho-hum about their faith. They do not have a close relationship to God and are unsure how to have one.

As a start they need to commit themselves to being the best disciples of Jesus Christ they can be. Then they should seek out some other Christians to disciple them. Although some believers can disciple themselves, most will need to get involved in the discipleship ministry of a local church or find some mature Christians who will disciple them. God uses human disciplers as well as His Spirit to encourage and mold lackadaisical believers into

Christ's image. Godly desires and intentions are where we have to begin, but to get to the end successfully, we need others to disciple us. Discipleship is the key to sustained and consistent growth.

We must either go forward and become serious about living the Christian life or stray further and further from God. Hebrews 2:1 says, "We must pay much closer attention to what we have heard, lest we drift away." If we begin to listen to and act on what we have heard from God, we will not wander away from Him and into deliberate sin with its terrible consequences (Heb. 2:2–3).

God wants to revitalize our lives, but we have to do whatever it takes to become His disciple. Becoming a commendable disciple of Jesus Christ does not happen overnight. In fact, it is a lifelong process of learning and growing. Yet if we are willing to pursue it properly, it will change our lives! And as our lives change, we will change the lives of others!

NOTES

INTRODUCTION

1. Edward E. Plowman, ed., *National and International Religion Report* 5, no. 11 (May 1991): 1.

CHAPTER 1

1. R. C. Sproul, *Pleasing God* (Wheaton, Ill.: Tyndale, 1988), 9.

2. Philip E. Hughes, *A Commentary on the Epistle to the Hebrews* (Grand Rapids, Mich.: Eerdmans, 1977), 189.

3. D. Edmond Hiebert, *The Thessalonian Epistles* (Chicago: Moody, 1971), 235.

4. Josh McDowell, *His Image . . . My Image* (San Bernardino, Calif.: Here's Life, 1984), 53–54.

5. Markus Barth, *Ephesians 4–6* (Garden City, N.J.: Doubleday, 1974), 506.

CHAPTER 2

1. F.F. Bruce, *I & II Thessalonians*, Word Biblical Commentary Series, eds. David A. Hubbard and Glenn W. Barker (Waco, Tex.: Word, 1983), 125.

2. A. T. Robertson, *A Grammar of the Greek New Testament in the Light of Historical Research*, (Nashville, Tenn.: Broadman, 1934), 890.

3. Mark Douglas Cain, "The Contribution of Philippians 2:12–13 to the Pauline Doctrine of Sanctification" (ThM thesis, Dallas Seminary, 1980), 30.

4. Walter Bauer, *A Greek-English Lexicon of the New Testament*, trans. William F. Arndt and F. Wilbur Gingrich (Chicago: University of Chicago, 1957), 265.

5. Cain, 46.

NOTES

CHAPTER 3

1. Ernest C. Reisinger, *The Carnal Christian* (London: Hazell Watson & Viney, n.d.), 20.

2. Sproul, 81.

3. David C. Needham, *Birthright* (Portland, Oreg.: Multnomah, 1979), 138.

4. Ibid., 139.

5. See Thomas Ice and Robert Dean, Jr., *A Holy Rebellion* (Eugene, Oreg.: Harvest, 1990) for a very thorough and biblical discussion of demons and spiritual warfare.

CHAPTER 4

1. Hiebert, 348.

2. Anne Ortland, *Children Are Wet Cement* (Old Tappan, N.J.: Revell, 1978), 155.

3. Fritz Rienecker, *A Linguistic Key to the Greek New Testament* (Grand Rapids, Mich.: Zondervan, 1980), 2:292.

4. J. I. Packer, *Hot Tub Religion* (Wheaton, Ill.: Tyndale, 1988), 199–200.

5. Leslie B. Flynn, *Come Alive with Illustrations* (Grand Rapids:Baker, 1987), 211.

CHAPTER 5

1. Keith Phillips, *The Making of a Disciple* (Old Tappan, N.J.: Revell, 1988), 13–14.

2. Bill Hull, *The Disciple-making Pastor* (Old Tappan, N.J.: Revell, 1988), 55.

3. Robert E. Coleman, *The Master Plan of Evangelism* (Old Tappan, N.J.: Revell, 1963), 48.

4. Phillips, 44.

5. Walter A. Hendrichsen, *Disciples Are Made—Not Born* (Wheaton, Ill.: Victor, 1974) 144–45.

6. Christopher B. Adsit, *Personal Discipleship Making* (San Bernardino, Calif.: Here's Life, 1988), 90.

7. Chuck Swindoll, *Dropping Your Guard* (Waco, Tex.: Word, 1983), 179.

8. Chuck Colson, *Presenting Belief in an Age of Unbelief* (Wheaton, Ill.: Victor, 1985), 29–30.

CHAPTER 6

1. Boyd Luter, "The Great Commission and the Church in Luke-Acts," *Evangelical Theological Society National Paper* (Nov. 1989).

2. Charles C. Ryrie, *So Great Salvation* (Wheaton, Ill.: Victor, 1989), 105.

3. Hiebert, 95.

4. Gary W. Kuhne, *The Dynamics of Personal Follow-up* (Grand Rapids, Mich.: Zondervan, 1976), 20.

5. Crabb and Allender, 91.

6. LeRoy Eims, *The Lost Art of Disciple Making* (Colorado Springs, Colo.: NavPress, 1978), 34.

7. Hiebert, 104.

8. Crabb and Allender, 71.

9. Hiebert, 104.

10. Ibid.

11. Acts 2:41; 8:36–37; 9:18; 10:44–48; 16:14–15, 32–33; 19:4–5.

12. Zane Hodges, *The Gospel Under Siege* (Dallas: Redencion Viva, 1981), 41.

PART 3 PROLOGUE

1. William Barker, *A Savior for All Seasons* (Old Tappan, N.J.: Revell, 1986), 111–12.

2. Barna Research Group, *The Church Today: Insightful Statistics and Commentary* (Barna Research Group, 1990), 29–30.

3. Packer, 202.

4. Ibid., 204.

CHAPTER 7

1. Dave Hunt, *The Cult Explosion* (Eugene, Oreg.: Harvest, 1980), 217.

2. Dennis J. DeHaan, *Windows on the Word* (Grand Rapids, Mich.: Baker, 1984), 12.

3. Leslie B. Flynn, *Great Church Fights* (Wheaton, Ill.: Victor, 1976), 16.

4. John F. MacArthur, Jr., *The Gospel According to Jesus* (Grand Rapids, Mich.: Zondervan, 1988), 22.

5. Ibid., 23.

6. Michael Green, ed., *Expositor's Illustrations File*, unpublished edition from Dallas Seminary, 1982.

CHAPTER 8

1. Richard Rice, *God's Foreknowledge and Man's Free Will* (Minneapolis, Minn.: Bethany, 1985), 21.

2. Harold S. Kushner, *When Bad Things Happen to Good People* (New York: Schocken, 1981), 43.

3. As quoted by Philip Yancey in *Disappointment With God* (Grand Rapids, Mich.: Zondervan, 1988), 179.

4. R. C. Sproul, *Surprised by Suffering* (Wheaton, Ill.: Tyndale, 1989), 189.

5. Bauer, 265.

6. Goldie Bristol, *When It's Hard to Forgive* (Wheaton, Ill.: Victor, 1982), 166.

7. V. Gilbert Beers, *Turn Your Hurts Into Healing* (Old Tappan, N.J.: Revell, 1988), 137.

CHAPTER 9

1. Yancey, 9.

2. See Robert Saucy, *The Church in God's Program* (Chicago: Moody, 1972), Chapter 5 in particular.

3. Charles Sell, *The House on the Rock* (Wheaton, Ill.: Victor, 1987), 16–17.

4. John Wimber and Kevin Springer, *Power Healing* (San Francisco: Harper & Row, 1987), 16.

5. Warren W. Wiersbe, *Why Us?* (Old Tappan, N.J.: Revell, 1984), 13.

6. John Wesley, Personal Journal, 1730.

7. Delores Kuenning, *Helping People Through Grief* (Minneapolis, Minn.: Bethany, 1987), 29.

8. Paul Lee Tan, *Encyclopedia of 7700 Illustrations* (Rockville, Md.: Assurance, 1979), 509.

CHAPTER 10

1. Gary Hardaway, "When Dreams Die," *Moody Monthly* 86 (June 1986), 20.

2. Wayne Grudem, *The Gift of Prophecy* (Westchester, Ill.: Crossway, 1988), 299.

3. See Part 3 Prologue for a fuller discussion of this subject.

4. Paul Little as quoted by Leslie Flynn and Bernice Flynn in *God's Will: You Can Know It* (Wheaton, Ill.: Victor, 1979), 97.

5. John Wesley, source unknown.

6. Grudem, 308.

7. D. A. Carson, *The Farewell Discourse and Final Prayer of Jesus* (Grand Rapids, Mich.: Baker, 1980), 74.

8. Donald Gee, *Spiritual Gifts in the Work of Ministry Today* (Tulsa, Okla.: Gospel, 1963), 51–52,

9. James Dobson, *Dr. Dobson Answers Your Questions* (Wheaton, Ill.: Tyndale, 1982), 477.

10. Garry Friesen, *Decision Making and the Will of God* (Portland, Oreg.: Multnomah, 1980), 143.

11. Ibid., 216.

12. Ibid., 223.

13. Ibid., 224.

14. Fred Market, "Active or Passive Lordship," Body Builder 4, no. 6 (Nov.-Dec. 1990), 3.

15. Walter Henrichsen and Gayle Jackson, *Applying the Bible* (Grand Rapids, Mich.: Zondervan, 1985), 197.

16. Larry Ward, "This Poor Man Cried...," in *My Most Memorable Encounter with God*, ed. David Enlow (Wheaton, Ill.: Tyndale, 1977), 215–17.

PART 4 PROLOGUE

1. John Naisbitt, *Megatrends* (New York: Warner, 1982), 147.

2. A. W. Tozer, *The Pursuit of God* (Wheaton, Ill.: Tyndale, n.d.), 69.

3. Bauer, 116*d*.

4. *Pulpit Helps*, Sept. 1986.

5. W. Mundle, "Godliness, Piety," in *The New International Dictionary of New Testament Words,* vol. 2, ed. Colin Brown (Grand Rapids, Mich.: Zondervan, 1976), 90–91.

CHAPTER 11

1. DeHaan, 18.

2. As reported in *USA Today,* 4 Jan. 1987.

3. *Our Daily Bread,* 17 June 1986.

4. Walter C. Kaiser, Jr., "What Is Biblical Meditation?" in *Renewing Your Mind in a Secular World*, ed. John D. Woodbridge (Chicago: Moody, 1985), 39–53.

5. Paul Meier, "Spiritual and Mental Health in the Balance," in Woodbridge, 27.

6. Sophie Laws, *The Epistle of James,* Harper's New Testament Commentaries, ed. Henry Chadwick (San Francisco: Harper & Row, 1980), 85.

7. James D. Davis, "Never a Purple Passage," *Des Moines (Iowa) Register,* 17 June 1986.

8. Source unknown.

CHAPTER 12

1. Green.

2. Gordon MacDonald, *Ordering Your Private World* (Nashville, Tenn.: Oliver-Nelson, 1984), 156.

3. George Müller, *Autobiography* (Pittsburgh, Penn.: Whitaker, 1984), 110.

4. DeHaan, 154.

5. D. L. Moody, *The Wit and Wisdom of D. L. Moody*, eds. Stanley and Patricia Gundry, (Chicago: Moody, 1974), 35.

6. Henri Nouwen, "The Spiritual Leader's Vitality," in *Leaders*, ed. Harold Myra (Waco, Tex.: Word, 1987), 46.

7. Howard Hendricks, *Taking a Stand* (Portland, Oreg.: Multnomah, 1979), 47–48.

CHAPTER 13

1. Jeanne Doering, *The Power of Encouragement* (Chicago: Moody, 1983), 113.

2. Mark McClosky, *Tell It Often—Tell It Well*, (San Bernardino, Calif.: Here's Life, 1985), 8.

3. Hull, 20.

4. *Common Ground* (Lutherville, Md.: Search Ministries, 1988), 1.

5. Joseph C. Aldrich, *Gentle Persuasion* (Portland, Oreg.: Multnomah, 1988), 243.

6. Tim Timmons, "Why Should They Listen to Me?" in*The Leadership Library*, vol. 8, *Preaching to Convince* , ed. James D. Berkley (Waco, Tex.: Word, 1985), 22.

7. As quoted by Joseph C. Aldrich in *Life-Style Evangelism* (Portland, Oreg.: Multnomah, 1981), 123.

8. Ibid., 83.

9. Donald L. Bubna, *Building People* (Wheaton, Ill.: Tyndale, 1978), 150.

10. Aldrich, *Life-Style Evangelism*, 227.

11. Tom Hanks as quoted by McCloskey, 207.

12. I personally recommend the Bad News–Good News approach of Evantell, which is an evangelical association "committed to expository evangelism." There are many good strategies, but I believe this one overall to be the best.

13. Paul E. Little, *How to Give Away Your Faith* (Downers Grove, Ill.: InterVarsity, 1973), Chapter 5.

14. Larry Moyer in *Toolbox*, Feb.–Apr. 1990: "the Gospel of John... exhorts us ninety-eight times to believe."

15. Bauer, 666.

16. Boyd Luter, *Anchor Bible Dictionary*, not yet published.

17. Leighton Ford, "Fear Is No Excuse," *Moody Monthly* 77 (July–Aug. 1977): 40–71.

18. Dawson Trotman, *Born to Reproduce* (Lincoln, Nebr.: Back to the Bible, n.d.), 19.

19. See for example Acts 1:8; 2 Corinthians 5:20; Matthew 28:19.

20. Green.

CHAPTER 14

1. Green.

2. Bauer, 439–40.

3. *Our Daily Bread,* 11 Oct. 1989.

4. Leslie B. Flynn, *Come Alive with Illustrations* (Grand Rapids, Mich.: Baker, 1987), 216.

5. Ronald Enroth, *The Lure of the Cults* (Downers Grove, Ill.: InterVarsity, 1979), 5.

6. Bauer, 439.

7. For what is meant by the term the "breaking of bread," see F. F. Bruce, *The Book of Acts* (Grand Rapids, Mich.: Eerdmans, 1988), 73.

8. Crabb and Allender, 98.

9. Quoted by Chuck Colson in *Kingdoms in Conflict* (Grand Rapids, Mich.: Zondervan, 1987), 44.

10. Bauer, 580.

CHAPTER 15

1. John Piper, *Desiring God* (Portland, Oreg.: Multnomah, 1986), 42.

2. Adapted from D. James Kennedy, *Evangelism Explosion* (Wheaton, Ill.: Tyndale, 1970), 30.

3. Jerry Jenkins, "For Starters," *Moody Monthly* 87 (Mar. 1987), 6.

4. MacArthur, 134.

5. "A Yummy MIL-F-14499F," *Time*, 6 Jan. 1986, 73.

6. S. Lewis Johnson, Jr., "How Faith Works," *Christianity Today,* 22 Sept. 1989, 25.

7. Edward E. Plowman, ed., *National and International Religion Report* 5, no. 19 (Sept. 1991): 6.

8. Some people believe that Hymenaeous is an indisputable example of a true believer who completely and permanently lost his faith (see Zane Hodges, *Absolutely Free* , pp. 108–111). However, this is a very questionable interpretation.

First of all, this interpretation depends heavily on a proposed similarity between Hymanaeous and the immoral man spoken about in 1 Cor. 5:15. It is true that both were "delivered over to Satan." However, the purposes were different. Paul delivered the immoral man over to Satan so that "his spirit may be saved in the day of the Lord Jesus" (1 Cor. 5:5). Hymanaeous and Alexander, on the other hand, were delivered over to Satan so that "they may be taught not to blaspheme." In other words, Paul believed that the immoral man would in the end be saved. But he does not state this about Hymenaeous. Paul only said that God wanted to teach him not to blaspheme, a purpose that God could have in regard to an unbeliever in order to cause repentance and faith.

Secondly, the understanding that Hymenaeous was a true Christian rests heavily on the interpretation of his "faith" as genuine (1 Tim. 1:20). But apparently this man's faith was not genuine. In 2 Timothy 2:17–18, Paul again discussed this man and stated that he went "astray from the truth." The word "astray" here can have the meaning "to miss the mark" (see Bauer, p. 117). Hymenaeous apparently never had genuine faith. He had "missed the mark," and his straying from the truth was inevitable. He appeared for a while to have embraced the truth, but he never really did so, and when he openly dismissed the truth, he took others with him who also never had genuine faith (v. 18).

In verse 19 Paul reminded us that, even when we cannot tell who is a true believer and who is not, "the Lord knows those who are His." This truth should not encourage us to sin, but rather to "abstain from wickedness." Paul goes on in verse 20 to explain that in a "large house," i.e., the Church, there are honorable vessels and dishonorable vessels. Thus, we should not be surprised that there are unbelievers mixed in with believers.

9. Sheldon Vanauken, *A Severe Mercy* (New York: Harper & Row, 1977), 191.

CHAPTER 16

1. David McCasland, "Restored," *Power for Living,* 12 Mar. 1989.

2. Moody, 60.

3. Hannah Whitall Smith, *The Christian's Secret of a Happy Life* (Old Tappan, N.J.: Revell, 1968).

4. J. B. Lightfoot, *The Epistle of St. Paul to the Galatians* (Grand Rapids, Mich.: Zondervan, 1956), 289.

5. David Frost and Michael Deakin, *David Frost's Book of the World's Worst Decisions* (New York: Crown, 1983), 26.

6. Hiebert, 238.

7. Ibid.

8. Bauer, 119b.

9. Hiebert, 350.

10. Geoffrey W. Bromiley, ed., *International Standard Bible Encyclopedia* (Grand Rapids, Mich.: Eerdmans, 1988), "Vine," by R. K. Harrison.

11 Joseph C. Dillow, "Abiding Is Remaining in Fellowship: Another Look at John 15:1–6," *Bibliotheca Sacra* 146 (Jan.–Mar. 1990): 55–66.

12. Bauer, 23–24.

13. 1 Corinthians 11:29–30; 1 Cor. 5:5; 1 John 5:16.

14. Hull, 93.

15. Robert Coleman, *The Master Plan of Discipleship* (Old Tappan, N.J.: Revell, 1987), 9.

SELECTED BIBLIOGRAPHY

Adsit, Christopher B. *Personal Discipleship Making.* San Bernardino, Calif.: Here's Life, 1988.

Aldrich, Joseph C. *Life-Style Evangelism.* Portland, Oreg.: Multnomah, 1981.

_____. *Gentle Persuasion.* Portland, Oreg.: Multnomah, 1988.

Barker, William. *A Savior for All Seasons.* Old Tappan, N.J.: Revell, 1986.

Barth, Markus. *Ephesians 4–6.* Garden City, N.J.: Doubleday, 1974.

Bauer, Walter. *A Greek-English Lexicon of the New Testament.* Translated by William F. Arndt and F. Wilbur Gingrich. Chicago: University of Chicago Press, 1957.

Beers, V. Gilbert. *Turn Your Hurts into Healing.* Old Tappan, N.J.: Revell, 1988.

Bristol, Goldie. *When It's Hard to Forgive.* Wheaton, Ill.: Victor, 1982.

Bromiley, Geoffrey W., ed. *International Standard Bible Encyclopedia.* "Vine," by R. K. Harrison. Grand Rapids, Mich.: Eerdmans,1988.

Brown, Colin, ed. *The New International Dictionary of New Testament Words.* Vol. 2. "Godliness, Piety," by W. Mundle. Grand Rapids, Mich.: Zondervan, 1976.

Bruce, F. F. *I & II Thessalonians.* Word Biblical Commentary Series, eds. David A. Hubbard and Glenn W. Barker. Waco, Tex.: Word, 1983.

Bruce, F. F. *The Book of Acts.* Grand Rapids, Mich.: Eerdmans, 1988.

Bubna, Donald L. *Building People.* Wheaton, Ill.: Tyndale, 1978.

Cain, Mark Douglas. "The Contribution of Philippians 2:12–13 to the Pauline Doctrine of Sanctification." ThM thesis, Dallas Seminary, 1980.

Carson, D. A. *The Farewell Discourse and Final Prayer of Jesus.* Grand Rapids, Mich.: Baker, 1980.

Coleman, Robert. *The Master Plan of Evangelism.* Old Tappan, N.J.: Revell, 1963.

_____. *The Master Plan of Discipleship.* Old Tappan, N.J.: Revell, 1987.

Colson, Charles. *Presenting Belief in an Age of Unbelief.* Wheaton, Ill.: Victor, 1985.

_____. *Kingdoms in Conflict.* Grand Rapids, Mich.: Zondervan, 1987.

Crabb, Lawrence J., Jr. and Dan B. Allender. *Encouragement.* Grand Rapids, Mich.: Zondervan, 1984.

DeHaan, Dennis J. *Windows on the Word.* Grand Rapids, Mich.: Baker, 1984.

Dillow, Joseph C. "Abiding Is Remaining in Fellowship: Another Look at John 15:1–6." *Bibliotheca Sacra* 146 (Jan.–Mar. 1990): 55–66.

Dobson, James. *Dr. Dobson Answers Your Questions.* Wheaton, Ill.: Tyndale, 1982.

Doering, Jeanne. *The Power of Encouragement.* Chicago: Moody, 1983.

Eims, LeRoy. *The Lost Art of Disciple Making.* Colorado Springs, Colo.: NavPress, 1978.

Enroth, Ronald. *The Lure of the Cults.* Downers Grove, Ill.: InterVarsity, 1979.

Flynn, Leslie B. *Come Alive with Illustrations.* Grand Rapids, Mich.: Baker, 1987.

Flynn, Leslie B. *Great Church Fights.* Wheaton, Ill.: Victor, 1976.

Ford, Leighton. "Fear Is No Excuse." *Moody Monthly* 77 (July–Aug. 1977): 40–42.

Friesen, Garry. *Decision Making and the Will of God.* Portland, Oreg.: Multnomah, 1980.

Gee, Donald. *Spiritual Gifts in the Work of Ministry Today.* Tulsa, Okla.: Gospel, 1963.

Green, Michael, ed. *Expositor's Illustrations File.* Unpublished edition from Dallas Seminary, 1992.

Grudem, Wayne. *The Gift of Prophecy.* Westchester, Ill.: Crossway, 1988.

Hendrichsen, Walter A. *Disciples Are Made—Not Born.* Wheaton, Ill.: Victor, 1974.

Hendrichsen, Walter A. and Gayle Jackson. *Applying the Bible.* Grand Rapids, Mich.: Zondervan, 1985.

Hendricks, Howard. *Taking a Stand.* Portland, Oreg.: Multnomah, 1979.

Hiebert, D. Edmond. *The Thessalonian Epistles.* Chicago: Moody, 1971.

Hodges, Zane C. *The Gospel Under Siege.* Dallas: Redencion Viva, 1981.

Hughes, Philip E. *A Commentary on the Epistle to the Hebrews.* Grand Rapids, Mich.: Eerdmans, 1977.

Hull, Bill. *The Disciple-Making Pastor.* Old Tappan, N.J.: Revell, 1988.

Hunt, David. *The Cult Explosion.* Eugene, Oreg.: Harvest, 1980.

Kaiser, Walter C., Jr. "What Is Biblical Meditation?" in *Renewing Your Mind*, ed. John D. Woodbridge. Chicago: Moody, 1985.

Kennedy, D. James. *Evangelism Explosion.* Wheaton, Ill.: Tyndale, 1970.

Kuenning, Delores. *Helping People Through Grief.* Minneapolis, Minn.: Bethany, 1987.

Kuhne, Gary W. *The Dynamics of Personal Follow-up*. Grand Rapids, Mich.: Zondervan, 1976.

Kushner, Harold S. *When Bad Things Happen to Good People*. New York: Schocken, 1981.

Laws, Sophie. *Epistle of James*. Harper's New Testament Commentaries, ed. Henry Chadwick. San Francisco: Harper & Row, 1980.

Lightfoot, J. B. *The Epistle of St. Paul to the Galatians*. Grand Rapids, Mich.: Zondervan, 1956.

Little, Paul. *How to Give Away Your Faith*. Downers Grove, Ill.: InterVarsity, 1973.

_____. Quoted by Leslie and Bernice Flynn in *God's Will: You Can Know It*. Wheaton, Ill.: Victor, 1979.

Luter, Boyd. "The Great Commission and the Church in Luke–Acts." *Evangelical Theological Society National Paper,* Nov. 1989.

_____. *Anchor Bible Dictionary*. Not yet published.

MacArthur, John F., Jr. *The Gospel According to Jesus*. Grand Rapids, Mich.: Zondervan, 1988.

MacDonald, Gordon. *Ordering Your Private World*. Nashville: Oliver-Nelson, 1984.

McClosky, Mark. *Tell It Often—Tell it Well*. With a Foreword by Bill Bright. San Bernardino, Calif.: Here's Life, 1985.

McDowell, Josh. *His Image . . . My Image*. San Bernardino, Calif.: Here's Life, 1984.

Meier, Paul. "Spiritual and Mental Health in the Balance." in *Renewing Your Mind in a Secular World*, ed. John D. Woodbridge. Chicago: Moody, 1985.

Moody, Dwight L. *The Wit and Wisdom of D. L. Moody*. Edited by Stanley Gundry and Patricia Gundry. Chicago: Moody, 1974.

Moyer, Larry. *You Can Tell It*. Dallas: EvanTell, Inc.

Müller, George. *Autobiography*. Pittsburgh, Penn.: Whitaker, 1984.

Naisbitt, John. *Megatrends*. New York: Warner, 1977.

Needham, David C. *Birthright*. Portland, Oreg.: Multnomah, 1979.

Nouwen, Henri. "The Spiritual's Leader's Vitality." In *Leaders,* ed. Harold Myra. Waco, Tex.: Word, 1987.

Ortland, Anne. *Children Are Wet Cement*. Old Tappan, N.J.: Revell, 1978.

Packer, J. I. *Hot Tub Religion*. Wheaton, Ill.: Tyndale, 1988.

Phillips, Keith. *The Making of a Disciple*. Old Tappan, N.J.: Revell, 1988.

Piper, John. *Desiring God*. Portland, Oreg.: Multnomah, 1986.

Reisinger, Ernest C. *The Carnal Christian*. London: Hazell Watson & Viney, n.d.

Rice, Richard. *God's Foreknowledge and Man's Free Will*. Minneapolis, Minn.: Bethany, 1985.

Rienecker, Fritz. *A Linguistic Key to the Greek New Testament*. Vol. 2. Grand Rapids, Mich.: Zondervan, 1980.

Robertson, A. T. *A Grammar of the Greek New Testament in the Light of Historical Research*. Nashville, Tenn.: Broadman, 1934.

Ryrie, Charles C. *So Great Salvation*. Wheaton, Ill.: Victor, 1989.

Saucy, Robert. *The Church in God's Program*. Chicago: Moody, 1972.

Sell, Charles. *The House on the Rock*. Wheaton, Ill.: Victor, 1987.

Smith, Hannah Whitall. *The Christian's Secret of a Happy Life*. Old Tappan, N.J.: Revell, 1968.

Sproul, R. C. *Pleasing God.* Wheaton, Ill.: Tyndale, 1988.

Swindoll, Chuck. *Dropping Your Guard.* Waco, Tex.: Word, 1983.

Tan, Paul Lee. *Encyclopedia of 7700 Illustrations.* Rockville, Md.: Assurance, 1979.

Timmons, Tim. "Why Should They Listen to Me?" In *The Leadership Library,* vol. 8, *Preaching to Convince,* ed. James D. Berkley. Waco, Tex.: Word, 1985.

Tozer, A. W. *The Pursuit of God.* Wheaton, Ill.: Tyndale, n.d.

Trotman, Dawson. *Born to Reproduce.* Lincoln, Nebr.: Back to the Bible Publications, n.d..

Vanauken, Sheldon. *A Severe Mercy.* New York: Harper & Row, 1977.

Ward, Larry. "This Poor Man Cried..." In *My Most Memorable Encounter with God,* ed. David Enlow. Wheaton, Ill.: Tyndale, 1977.

Wesley, John. *Personal Journal.* 1730.

Wiersbe, Warren W. *Why Us?* Old Tappan, N.J.: Revell, 1984.

Wimber, John and Kevin Springs. *Power Healing.* San Francisco: Harper & Row, 1987.

Wright, Norman. *More Communication Keys to Your Marriage.* Ventura, Calif.: Regal, 1983.

Yancey, Philip. *Disappointment with God.* Grand Rapids, Mich.: Zondervan, 1988.

NOTE TO THE READER

The publisher invites you to share your response to the message of this book by writing Discovery House Publishers, P.O. Box 3566, Grand Rapids, MI 49501, U.S.A. or by calling 1-800-283-8333. For information about other Discovery House publications, contact us at the same address and phone number.